Steering Clear
Of
Highway Madness

Steering Clear
Of
Highway Madness

A Driver's Guide To Curbing Stress And Strain

John A. Larson, M.D.

BookPartners, Inc.
Wilsonville, Oregon

BookPartners gratefully acknowledges the songmasters of two American favorites, lines from "The Sunny Side Of The Street" and "Moonlight Bay" which are reproduced in the text.

"The Sunny Side Of The Street," Published 1930.
Words by: Dorothy Fields
Music by: Jimmy McHugh
Company: Musical Theatre.

"Moonlight Bay," Published 1912.
Words by: Percy Wenrich
Music by: Edward Madden
Company: Victor.

BookPartners, Inc.
P.O. Box 922
Wilsonville, Oregon 97070

Dedication

To my dad
Edwin Renius Larson
who taught me both the stress
and the joy of driving.

Acknowledgements

First, to my wife, Patricia MacQueen, whose commitment, love and support empowered me throughout the six years of writing and rewriting. Second, to Herbert Freudenberger, Ph.D., whose wisdom, example and cleverness enabled me to overcome my aversion to taking a stand. Third, to my children, Chris, Karen and John, who suffered me through my tempestuous years, and have loved me no matter what; and to Leo, Patricia's son, whose courage and willingness to dare inspired me.

Many have read earlier drafts and made constructive and valuable suggestions including my brother, Edwin Larson, M.D., and Harold Grinspoon, Frank Hall, Rich Zelisko, M.S.W., Lou Fierman, M.D., Ella Fierman, M.S.W., Thelma Jean Goodrich, Ph.D., and Ida Davidoff, Ed.D.

My teacher, Mike Friedman, M.D., made this whole endeavor possible through his brilliant early insights; I appreciate his confidence in me by allowing part of the Coronary/Cancer Research Project to be under my direction in Norwalk. I learned much from the other group leaders: Fred Drews, Ph.D., Susan Shavin, Ph.D., Barbara Powell, Ph.D., and Janet Anderson, R.N.

I am grateful for the constant support of Richard Sallick, M.D., Chief of Psychiatry at Norwalk Hospital, and to the administrators who, early on, recognized the value and provided me space to do my work: Jim Arenholz, Fred Schiavo and Patrick Neligan, M.D. My thanks also to Barbara Klein, Bruce Hutchinson and Maura Romaine for promoting the research to the community.

None of this could have happened without the collaboration of the Department of Medicine and the Section of Cardiology at Norwalk Hospital. Cardiologists Marshal Franklin, M.D. and Mark Lichtman, M.D., along with the nurse who became first director of cardiac rehabilitation, Rebecca Marcus, R.N., invited me to consult on the formation of cardiac rehabilitation in 1972. Martin Floch, M.D., Chief of Medicine, encouraged my work, and Martin Krauthamer, M.D., Chief of Cardiology, along with cardiologists Ralph Kirmser, M.D., Robert Moskowitz, M.D., Karl Alcan, M.D., Abe Bornstein, M.D., George Nelson, M.D., Jonathan Greenwald, M.D., Steve Michelson, M.D., Tao-Nan Chi, M.D., Charles Augenbraun, M.D., Jesus Yap, M.D., and the current director of cardiac rehabilitation, Patty Biancini-Wolk, R.N., have entrusted me with the treatment of their patients.

My thanks to Joseph Andrews, M.D., Chief of Staff at Norwalk Hospital, for going to bat for prevention treatment programs. My gratitude also to my colleagues in Stress Medicine, psychiatrists Frank Hamilton, M.D., Robert Israel, M.D. and George Kelly, M.D., and to social workers Anita Galvan, M.S.W. and Anne Ford, M.S.W.

Judith Brown, Jan Mello, Doreen Cohn and Leslie Sweet were indispensable in editing and preparing various stages of the manuscript. Thorn Bacon, my editor at BookPartners, elevated the book to new dimensions through his insightful suggestions, and Ursula Bacon created the artistic accompaniment with her cover design.

I hope my respect and admiration for the members of the treatment groups comes through. The ideas presented here were not developed in isolation, but in a continuing dialogue with all of them, fellow travelers on this planet.

John Larson, M.D.
Norwalk, CT
February 10, 1996

Table Of Contents

Foreword

I became somewhat sad while reading Dr. Larson's *Steering Clear of Highway Madness* because I kept remembering that 50,000 Americans lost their lives during 1994 in automobile accidents, and that thousands already have died in 1995 in the same fashion. Half of the deaths could have been prevented if the impatience and free-floating hostility (the two overt components responsible for Type A behavior) afflicting these drivers had been eliminated.

These two components of Type A behavior which are sickening drivers can be eliminated as we now are doing in our ongoing Type A counseling groups, of which Dr. Larson is a participating counselor. In writing this book he has outlined some of the important changes in the belief systems of Type A drivers which must be accomplished if they are to enjoy driving their cars anywhere, anytime.

If the contents of this book were read and acted upon by the millions of American Type A drivers, the number of deaths prevented each year would easily surpass by five times the number of deaths from AIDS. Yes, this is a book that has been needed for more than five decades to cure an illness that has "tolled the bell" for so many thousands of Americans.

Meyer Friedman, M.D.
San Francisco, California

Preface

In his compelling book *Steering Clear of Highway Madness,* Dr. Larson has presented in concise and readable form a menace which lies lurking in our society — highway hostility and stress.

He defines five types of personalities that ride the roads and their consequent destructive behavior to themselves and others. The five are: the Speeder, the Competitor, the Passive/Aggressor, the Narcissist and the Vigilante.

In each chapter Dr. Larson presents the personal dynamics of such individuals. He delineates, through entertaining and enlightening anecdotes, each group. The thoughtful presentations are accompanied by a discussion on values, both individual and societal. One value that deserves discussion is the value of needing to compete. As Dr. Larson indicates, "American culture enshrines competing as a value not to be questioned." The author does question. However, his questioning revolves around our manner of thinking, perceiving, sensing and relating to time. The chapters are uniform in presenting old beliefs and new beliefs involving each personality. These groupings are accompanied by a description of the "stressors," and the events precipitating improper driving. The author cites six to eight illustrations in each case to allow the reader to begin to identify and associate these stress reactions to himself or herself.

A novel approach that Dr. Larson has presented is the use of memorization cards to assist in curbing highway hostility. These may be used to reinforce one's thoughts after re-evaluating one's beliefs.

A poignant comment that is presented over and over is that these personality categories may, at the minimum lead to internal stressors, coronaries or eventual death.

The most ideal application of this book is that it ought to be "assigned" as part of driver education courses in the high schools; and ought to be viewed as "must" reading for those who are found to have serious traffic violations.

It is a seminal book which describes a "new" area of stress that has been minimally attended to — highway hostilities and fatalities. It was a pleasure to read and is written in a straightforward, honest and learned style.

Herbert J. Freudenberger, Ph.D.
New York, N.Y.

Introduction

As a boy in the early 1930s, I remember riding in cars before they had heaters. In the cold Wisconsin winters, we bundled up and covered our laps with blankets whenever we'd take a trip. Being on the road was a glorious adventure!

First, was the thrill of being transported at speeds not otherwise attainable. Then came the delight of viewing the ever-changing panorama on both sides of the car. How interesting to see such diversity of beauty! I never knew what to expect.

It was fun anticipating our arrival at familiar destinations: Grandmother's farm, Taylor's Falls, Balsam Lake, and visiting with "distant" relatives who lived in St. Paul, thirty-six miles away. I felt special when my father took me along while he visited area farmers to whom he sold machinery. I'll always remember him singing to me "Moonlight Bay," "Sweet Adeline," "My Wild Irish Rose," and other tunes on the way home.

Of course, the unexpected happened: flat tires, getting stuck in snow, pulling through the muddy ruts of new construction, encounters with chickens, cows, hay wagons, horses, and billows of dust from passing cars, all of which presented ordinary hazards.

But while being on the road was a joy to me, it was often stressful to my father. When making distant trips he was obsessed with "making good time," and he set daily mileage goals that strained the endurance of his children, not to mention his patient wife. My father battled other cars to reach his goals, creating tension and irritation. He turned what should have been an adventurous, joyful journey into an anxiety-filled competition!

When I began driving — an exercise I love — I drove like my dad: fast, setting rigorous driving goals, and I became furious at the "stupidity" of some drivers.

I never thought there was anything wrong with my attitude. Later, during my psychiatric residency at The Menninger Clinic, interested in what was then called psychosomatic medicine, I discovered that attitudes affect health. I particularly admired the theories of Franz Alexander, a Chicago psychoanalyst, who suggested that emotional states cause illness.

In 1963, while Chief of Psychiatry at Springfield Hospital in Springfield, Massachusetts, I was asked to consult on the case of a thirty-four-year-old insurance salesman, who had had a heart attack. He had stressed himself with his bottled-up anger, his ferocious striving and his hectic pace. Though at the time I did not question him about his driving habits, I have no doubt — judging from my experience treating more than 1,000 men with heart attacks — that he "battled" traffic much as my father did.

Alexander's theories about the role of the psyche in

heart attacks began to make more sense. From that day, over thirty years ago, until this moment, the prevention of heart attacks by psychological intervention has been my primary professional interest.

Concurrent with my meeting the salesman, two cardiologists in San Francisco, Dr. Meyer Friedman and Dr. Raymond Rosenman, were conducting research that was to prove a strong link between Type A men — those who were quick to get angry, irritated, aggravated, or impatient at the slightest provocation (including highway frustrations) and their propensity for heart attack.

Since 1984, after having learned successful behavior modification techniques at the Friedman Institute, I have treated coronary-prone individuals at the Institute of Stress Medicine at Norwalk Hospital, in Norwalk, Connecticut.

My studies have taught me that men and women who have had heart attacks tend to overreact to events that happen while they're driving. Early in group treatment this overreaction to highway stressors becomes the focus for behavioral change. Cognitive therapy treatment techniques, like those described in this book, have been applied with considerable success. Patients become calmer, less angry drivers.

In the process of helping my patients prevent heart attacks, I have become knowledgeable about highway stress in general, and, most important, how to reduce it.

Hence, this book is intended to enable you to change your own attitudes which may cause you to overreact to highway stressors. When you alter these attitudes and beliefs, you will lower the duration, frequency, and intensity of your tension while you are driving. As your stress reaction lowers, so will the chances of your having a heart attack or other stress-related illness.

One last important point: this book is meant as a treatment book. Anyone who reads, understands, and does the exercises should experience less anger while driving. Since repetition and reinforcement is necessary for learning, words and phrases are repeated and paraphrased throughout the text.

In order to gauge how well this works, I urge you to take the Driver's Stress Profile, Chapter 2. Be honest with your answers. Then, after reading the book, doing the exercises and practicing on the road for one month, retake the test as shown again in Chapter 16 without looking at your previous results. Be honest at that point, too. Three months after reading this book, you should see further improvement.

I believe you will find that your highway anger is reduced, your driving safety enhanced, and your enjoyment of your journeys on the road increased.

1

Handmaidens Of Highway Injury And Death

"Be Prepared."

Boy Scout Motto

Highway injury and death come from violence, accidents, and stress illness. At first glance these three phenomena may seem to be quite different, but more than thirty years of studying stress convinces me they are linked by emotional states growing out of five common attitudes present to various degrees in all drivers. I choose to think of these attitudes as the handmaidens of highway injury and death.

Evidence shows that when these attitudes are challenged by frustrating highway events, strong emotional states characterized by rage, anger, resentment, impatience, and anxiety are triggered. Like water heated to the boiling point, flaring emotions can overwhelm the driver's judgement, leading to violence and risky driving behaviors. When they become chronic and repetitive, these emotions which I call *Highway Madness,* can lead to pathological changes within the driver's body. The result is disease.

Highway Madness, defined: Short periods of irrational thoughts, feelings and behavior, lasting from seconds to hours and characterized predominately by feelings of intense anger and rage triggered by either another driver's behavior or a road condition. During this time period drivers:

1. Experience exaggerated anger, irritation, aggravation and impatience focusing on the most trivial occurrences;
2. Become preoccupied with thoughts about what happened, distracting them from their driving, leaving them vulnerable to new dangers;
3. Form irrational convictions about the personality and motivations of the other driver, based on flimsy evidence;
4. Experience impaired judgement, saying or doing things they later regret, including engaging in risky driving behaviors themselves, while attempting to punish or retaliate against the offending driver;
5. Suffer from diminished sensibilities, i.e. their ability to hear, see, feel, touch, smell and taste is dulled.
6. Lose brain capacity, the power of abstract thinking, empathy, humor, appreciation of beauty and the ability to feel love.

If we understand the mental mechanisms involved in the chain of events leading to hostile driver behavior, prevention of many highway calamities becomes possible. Unquestionably, as our nation's roads become more crowded with impatient drivers jostling for space and advantage, angry encounters will become more common, and more deadly. We must adapt to new ways of thinking — new ways that will prompt us to *Steer Clear Of Highway Madness!*

Each driver has within his power the ability to change his attitudes without any negative affect on his driving and his arrival time at his destination. With the change in perception that develops from these new driving attitudes comes a new joy behind the wheel and a sense of freedom and satisfaction the driver may have thought lost to him. Not only will driving be more relaxed, enjoyable and free of hostility, but chances of accidents will be significantly reduced. Violence will drop through changes in policing practices and increased community involvement in safe motoring.

To convince you that what I'm suggesting is practical, very "doable" for the average driver, (not to mention the fact that it may save your life) I wish, first, to make you better acquainted with the raw data of highway hostility. Next, we'll start our journey of prevention by examining the different attitudes that motivate pugnacious driving and move on to the simple but effective methods to alter these destructive attitudes permanently.

VIOLENCE

That our highways have become uncertain and dangerous is not news. I should know, for even though I am a physician and an expert in stress medicine, I was an angry driver before I discovered the harm I was doing to myself and the high risk of traffic mayhem I was contributing to by my "get-out-of-the-way" attitude. The following reports are examples of driver frustration beyond the breaking point. They are culled from articles published across the country.

THE MADDENING KISS

Michelle and Darren, newlyweds, halted at a Houston stop sign, and paused to kiss before proceeding toward their honeymoon destination. The man in the white car behind them became enraged at the delay, leaned on his horn, pulled around in front of them, jumped out of his vehicle and began pounding on their window, shouting expletives at Michelle, who was driving.

He didn't respond as Michelle pointed at the gaily decorated "Just Married" sign. Darren got out of the car to calm the man, but was wrestled to the ground and stabbed in the abdomen. The irate assailant fled in his car. Darren recovered, but spent three days in the hospital.

FATAL BUMP

Oscar Salinas, driving with his friend, Joaquin, in Houston, Texas, tried to stop, but poor brakes failed and his auto tapped the rear bumper of a pickup truck. No damage was done, and Oscar drove away, but the pickup followed. The driver pulled abreast of the car and someone inside the truck cab shot and killed Oscar, critically wounding Joaquin.

A BROKEN ARM

In Houston, Allen Wilder's car stalled in the middle of a jammed freeway. He couldn't get it started. Behind him, the driver of a dump truck became aggravated and rammed Wilder viciously. Then, still steaming, he jumped out of the truck with a steel bolt and began to beat on the trunk of

Allen's car. When Allen tried to stop the mayhem, the truck driver struck Allen's forearm, breaking it, then drove off when another driver yelled at him.

RECORD OF ASSAULTS

During one ten-month period in Houston, there were 161 formal complaints of violent altercations, from fist fights to fatal shootings, as a result of driving frustration.

During the summer of 1987, in Los Angeles County, there were 137 incidents of highway assaults with firearms. Eighty-three shootings occurred, resulting in seventeen injuries, including two fatalities!

The highway events triggering the confrontations were lane changing, merging, tailgating, speeding, and impeding traffic.

VOLKSWAGEN DRIVER KILLED

Shocked Los Angeles neighbors described seventeen-year-old Russell Joseph Pirrone as a "happy-go-lucky kid who was very affectionate to his family."

"You can't say enough nice things about him. He was a really good kid. He took newspapers to the church every week."

Russell and a buddy decided to take a break from cleaning an apartment and get a hamburger one Friday evening. Driving Russell's Volkswagen beetle, they cut in front of a pick-up truck, then stopped at the next light.

Russell's friend recalled what happened next: "We hung a right. The traffic was still coming. They honked directly behind us, and called us names. Then, they pulled up on the side. They went a little forward, then slowed down. I heard a noise, and looked up and saw the guy with a gun in his hand. We still continued to go forward after Russell was shot, but we started to slow down."

Russell was taken to Pomona Valley hospital, where he was pronounced dead.

PARALYZED BY BULLET

The congested traffic crept along about 7:00 P.M. on a Saturday night near the terminus of the Newport-Costa Mesa Freeway in the Greater Los Angeles area. Paul Gary Nusbaum, a twenty-eight-year-old Rolling Hills Estates man, driving alone, became involved in a right-of-way dispute with another car driven by Albert Carroll Morgan, a thirty-two-year-old roofer from Santa Ana.

Morgan became enraged at Nusbaum, and shot him in the neck. Nusbaum's car went out of control and slammed into three other cars.

He was taken to the Fountain Valley Medical Center's intensive care unit in critical condition. Paul Nusbaum is paralyzed.

KILLED ON THE FREEWAY

Eighteen-year-old Sandra Leigh Tate, traveling on the Santa Ana Freeway fast lane, failed to pull over when the car behind tailgated her. The driver flashed his lights. Still Sandra refused to pull over.

"Just all of a sudden, there he was — so close I couldn't even see the headlights," she recalled.

Suddenly, the driver veered and passed Sandra on the right. As he came even with her passenger side window where Sandra's boyfriend, Rich Bynum sat, the man raised a .38 caliber pistol and shot twice, striking Rich in the neck both times.

Rich died.

VAN DRIVER'S WIFE KILLED

Harold Harvey Hawks didn't pull over fast enough for the driver of a van one night on the Riverside Freeway in California. Furious, the van's driver flashed his bright lights, and when Hawks still didn't budge, he drove alongside Hawks' car, threw a can at him then drew ahead of Hawks, cutting him off. The van driver's action inflamed Hawks who later said he just wanted to scare the driver of the van when he pulled out a 12-gauge shotgun and fired.

The pellets from the blast hit Patricia Dwyer, an off-duty Corona policewoman who was sitting next to her husband, the van driver. She was killed.

Harold was arrested, tried and convicted of second degree murder.

The jury forewoman, Joyce Beck, summed up the evidence, "Two hotheads met on the highway, and neither one of them would give in."

HIGHWAY HOSTILITY WIDESPREAD

Texas and California drivers do not have a monopoly on highway mayhem. Weapons and violence are just as visible in Detroit, where, in a recent year, between November and February, twenty-eight highway shootings were reported.

An Illinois state highway patrol office reports receiving two or three calls each day about altercations between motorists. State Trooper Ty Kansaki comments:

"The most minor traffic accident leads people to slug it out." Kansaki has avowed that he will no longer go on patrol without his bulletproof vest. "We're just trying to keep them from hurting and killing each other."

In Louisiana, State Trooper Mike Taylor characterizes altercations between motorists as the "Jekyll-and-Hyde syndrome." According to Taylor, otherwise normal citizens lose their heads over minor blacktop annoyances. "People who get caught up in these incidents seem to go nuts," he said.

But, he added, "In sixteen years on the job, I've found that if a guy is overly emotional and extremely upset, once you get him out of the car he calms down."

In Denver, the statistics on highway madness indicate that Rocky Mountain drivers are not immune to the highway hostility virus: During a three year period, four motorists were shot to death and six seriously injured after unrelated traffic altercations.

"We know it wasn't summer that did it — the heat and temperature and all — because a lot of it was in the winter," said Denver Police Detective John Wyckoff.

In San Francisco, at least seven violent incidents among drivers, including one death, happened within one month. Three occurred on the Bay Bridge, a bumper to bumper span between San Francisco and Oakland, and three others took place near San Francisco International Airport when repaving operations snarled traffic and elevated tempers.

In Portland, 600 miles north, between November and February, 1993, police received more than sixty reports of projectiles smashing into windows. One man waited trial for attempted murder when he allegedly shot a bullet through the window of a taxicab.

Dr. Ronald Turco, a psychiatrist who works part time as a detective with the Newberg, New York Police Department said, "I'm just extremely cautious when I'm driving. When somebody cuts me off, I just let them go because they could pull out a gun. I don't argue with anybody. It's just too crazy. It used to be years ago you could shake a fist and let some steam off, but now you can't."

AUTOMOBILE ACCIDENTS: A BRIEF HISTORY

On an international scale, London has the title for being the first city in the world in which a person was killed by an automobile. It happened in August, 1896, at Crystal Palace in South London. Mrs. Bridget Driscoll became the first victim of a car, according to Marsh and Collett as reported in their book, *Driving Passion.* Three years later, Mr. Henry Bliss became the first to suffer the same fate in the United States.

In 1951, Mrs. Elma Wischmeir became the millionth American killed on the road. By 1986, the fatality rate had climbed so high that a record thirty-seven people in the United States died each year for every 100,000 cars on the road. In Belgium and Germany, the figure is four times as high. Israel and Greece have the highest auto fatality rate in the world: 200 and 195 deaths respectively per 100,000 vehicles.

To give greater meaning to the statistics, the *Journal of the American Medical Association* in September 1994, reported that 6,000 persons aged sixteen to twenty died from motor vehicle crashes in 1991, twice as many as from any other cause of death among persons in this age group.

The same JAMA article observed that, "Young drivers

account disproportionately for motor vehicle crashes worldwide, reflecting, in part, the combination of immaturity and lack of driving experience. Adolescent drivers are more apt than adult drivers to resort to speeding, running red lights, making illegal turns, not wearing safety belts, riding with an intoxicated driver, and driving after using drugs or alcohol."

According to Professor Ray Fuller of the University of Dublin, "A Swedish study of speeds on narrow winding roadways showed that drivers ultimately learn to travel at such a speed that, should an obstruction occur around the next bend, they would have no chance of avoiding a collision."

"Such behavioral traps arise," he said, "because the contingency between a particularly rewarding driving behavior (traveling at a high speed) and a hazardous consequence is improbable and uncertain."

It is more and more obvious that as the world grows more crowded and highways more cluttered, injuries and fatalities will increase alarmingly as a result of drivers' destructive attitudes. Dr. James Malfetti, executive officer of the Safety Education Project at Columbia University, describes states of mind that contribute to the death and injury statistics: "The social deviate and the normal individual looking for a change of pace commit the same type of driving errors. They both invite accidents. In extreme cases either one can be described as an accident riding around looking for a place to happen."

Aggressive attitudes on the road can be triggered by a non-driving incident. This was pointed out by authors O'Connell and Myers in their book, *Safety Last,* in which they cited a businessman who had driven safely in Manhatten for eleven years. One day his boss overlooked him for a promotion, making it impossible for him to move his family to a better neighborhood. The next day, he slapped his little daughter at breakfast, something he had never done before, and was sideswiped on the way to work as he tried to beat a light.

Another excerpt from the book describes a disturbed husband: "I was upset that day because my wife went out to stay with some people. We had a fight. I was going back to the base. I was thinking about my wife. I saw the light changing from green to amber, but I thought I could make it. They say I hit a car coming through the intersection. I guess I should have been paying more attention."

The need to modify drivers' attitudes nationally and internationally was demonstrated by a report on Portugal appearing in the *New York Times* in May, 1991: "Driving is Portugal's number one public health problem," said Major Gabriel Mendes, the deputy commander of the country's Transit Brigade. "People behave very differently when they are in the driver's seat from what they do in ordinary life."

The Portuguese have the reputation of being a quiet, law-abiding and introverted people, who, even in times of political turmoil, go out of their way to avoid using violence. But, mysteriously, when they get into their cars, they are aggressive and dangerous," Major Mendes said.

"In Lisbon, they careen up and down the city's steep hills, immune to the presence of pedestrians or other drivers. Outside the capital, their specialty seems to be over-taking on blind corners, a problem aggravated by the fact that the country still has only 200 miles of modern highways. The death rate on Portugal's roads is consistently the highest within the twelve-nation European Community. Measured in relation to total vehicles, it is four times higher than Britain, the Netherlands, and the United States."

Contributing to the international obsession with fast cars are the automobile advertisers, who clearly understand the fascination with speed on the highways as an escape from normalcy.

In their book, *Driving Passion,* authors Marsh and Collett note how car names encourage aggressive and belligerent highway attitudes. Consider "Jaguar — named after a ferocious South American beast of prey. Mustang — a wild untamable beast. Cougar, Bronco, Panther, Taurus, Firebird, and Thunderbird — fast and violent animals, real or imaginary."

Cars named after sharp-edged weapons in Britain include the Scimitar, Rapier, and Dart, and in the United States, Cutlass and Le Sabre. Violent phenomena of nature are transformed into powerful automobile images with names like Fuego, Duster and Tornado.

William Haddon, head of the Insurance Institute for Highway Safety in Washington, D.C., was quoted in *Driving Passion* on the subject of inflammatory names for autos: "There is — the glaring discrepancy between the need of societies to reduce motor vehicle casualties — and the images of violence and machismo with which many of the vehicles are sold; images which it is reasonable to believe increase the occurrence of motor vehicle death and maiming...."

How drivers' attitudes affect their safe performance behind the wheel is the subject of a statement in the September 1995 issue of the American Automobile Association's journal, *Car and Driver.* A lead article quotes driving safety consultant Dr. Francis Kenel, who found, "Those drivers who exhibited extremes of over-control and under-control had horrendous driving records. Their attitudes adversely affected how they handled the car."

CRUISING FOR A HEART ATTACK

Deadly as inappropriate attitudes can be for public driving, the health and safety of motorists can be severely affected by their own anger and frustration. Persistent and repeated episodes of outrage while driving can, indeed, induce heart attacks. Since 1975, I have interviewed over 1,000 patients with heart attacks at Norwalk Hospital. Eighty percent of them had a long history of violent anger or outrage behind the wheel. The association is clear: temper outbursts (or inbursts) can precede coronary thrombosis.

The association between heart attack and rage was first observed at the Friedman Institute in San Francisco. While engaged in a long-term study of the behavioral and psychophysiologic precursors to heart attacks, Dr. Friedman and his fellow cardiologist, Dr. Rosenman, discovered in heart attack patients an "emotional complex" designated by a "behavior pattern of competitiveness, excessive drive, and an enhanced sense of time urgency." They dubbed it, "the hurry sickness," and this behavior pattern occurred in all aspects of a person's life, including driving.

From 1960 to 1969, Friedman and Rosenman embarked on a study of 3,200 men. These men, free of any apparent disease at the beginning of the research, were individually interviewed to see if they had the "hurry sickness." Those who did were identified as Type A; and those who didn't, Type B.

During the eight-year period, the men under study began having heart attacks and it was discovered that most of the victims were those men with the "hurry sickness." The Type As had almost three times the frequency of heart attacks as the Type Bs.

In their 1974 book, *Type A Behavior and Your Heart,* the researchers expanded on their description of the psychophysiologic state to include four key markers, which, when present in an individual, may lead to heart attack: Anger, Irritation, Aggravation, Impatience.

When these emotions are felt long enough, frequently enough, and intensely enough, an individual is apt to have a heart attack if he is genetically predisposed.

Can these behavior patterns be changed? The Friedman Institute sought to answer this important question in a 1983 report entitled, "The Recurrent Coronary Prevention Project." Eight hundred sixty-two men who had survived one heart attack enrolled in the research. They were divided into two groups; one group attended regular sessions to help them curb their hostility, the other group did not. After three years the number of new heart attacks in each group was tallied. The difference in the recurrent rate was dramatic: those receiving hostility aversion treatment had forty-four percent fewer myocardial infarctions than the non-treated group.

What's more, of those who were engaged in the hostility reduction group, and who had had coronary artery by-pass following their first heart attack prior to entering the study, sixty percent had fewer new heart attacks than the untreated group. In the course of treatment, it became apparent that impatience and temper while driving occurred in most heart attack patients. Treatment techniques, described later in this book, were developed to reduce such temperamental outbursts. These proved to be surprisingly effective, and became a regular feature of treatment strategies, usually at an early stage.

Other researchers have confirmed the Friedman Institute's findings, most notably Dr. Redford Williams, professor of psychiatry and director of the Behavioral Medicine Research Center at Duke University. In his 1989 book, *The Trusting Heart,* Williams concluded that "...anger has a real biological cost...for subjects with high hostility."

In 1993, Williams was able to state, with even greater authority in the book, *Anger Kills,* written with his wife, Dr. Virginia Williams, "About 20 percent of the general population has levels of hostility high enough to be dangerous to health. Another 20 percent has very low levels, and the rest fall somewhere in between."

The third researcher who has contributed heavily to our understanding of stress on the heart confirmed the discoveries of Friedman and Williams. He is Dr. Dean Ornish, and in his book, *Reversing Heart Disease,* he concludes: "In summary, then, emotional stress can lead to heart disease and other illnesses. Stress comes not only from what we do, but how we react to the external world. How we react, in turn, is based on how we perceive ourselves in relation to the world."

It was Dr. Ornish who demonstrated that partially clogged coronary arteries can begin to open, relieving disabling heart symptoms, when a person follows a program of stress reduction, attitudinal change, meditation, increase in the quality of relationships, and eats a low fat diet.

Attitudinal changes are the basis for reducing stress and strain, and since much of aggressive behavior in our society takes place behind the wheel of a car, modification of the manner in which a person views his driving, and other motorists, can not only reduce stress leading to heart attack, but can help the driver minimize madness on the highways.

In the next chapters you will become better acquainted with men and women like you and me, who have attitudes that may lead to bodily stress and highway confrontation if not altered. You may see yourself in some of these people. I hope you'll discover that life on the highway can be a less dangerous and more rewarding adventure.

2

Driver's Stress Profile

Take the test before reading the book and one month after reading the book, memorizing the new beliefs and practice, practice, practice.

Answer each statement as honestly as you can. See pages 27 and 28 for scoring information. Score each statement that applies to you as follows:

Always - 3 — Often - 2 — Sometimes - 1 — Never - 0

I	Anger	Score
1.	Get angry at drivers.	_____
2.	Get angry at fast drivers.	_____
3.	Get angry at slow drivers.	_____
4.	Get angry when cut off.	_____
5.	Get angry at malfunctioning stoplights.	_____
6.	Get angry at traffic jams.	_____
7.	Spouse or friends tell you to calm down.	_____

8. Get angry at tailgaters. _____
9. Get angry at your passengers. _____
10. Get angry when multilane highway narrows. _____
    Total I: _____

II   Impatience

1. Impatient waiting for passengers to get in. _____
2. So impatient, won't let car engine warm up. _____
3. Impatient at stoplights. _____
4. Impatient waiting in lines (car wash, bank). _____
5. Impatient waiting for parking space. _____
6. As passenger, impatient with driver. _____
7. Impatient when car ahead slows down. _____
8. Impatient if behind schedule on a trip. _____
9. Impatient driving in far right, slow lane. _____
10. Impatient with pedestrians crossing street. _____
    Total II: _____

III   Competing

1. Compete on the road. _____
2. Compete with yourself. _____
3. Compete with other drivers. _____
4. Challenge other drivers. _____
5. Race other drivers. _____
6. Compete with cars in tollbooth lines. _____
7. Compete with other cars in traffic jams. _____
8. Compete with drivers who challenge you. _____
9. Compete to amuse self when bored. _____
10. Drag race adjacent car at stop lights. _____
    Total III: _____

IV   Punishing

1.   Do you "punish" bad drivers. ____
2.   Complain to passengers about other drivers. ____
3.   Curse at other drivers. ____
4.   Make obscene gestures. ____
5.   Block cars trying to pass. ____
6.   Block cars trying to change lanes. ____
7.   Ride another car's tail. ____
8.   Brake suddenly to punish tailgater. ____
9.   Use high beams to punish bad driver. ____
10. Seek personal encounter with bad driver. ____
     Total IV: ____

Total of I, II, III, IV ____

SIGNIFICANCE OF DRIVER'S STRESS PROFILE

Answering honestly and accurately, you can obtain a measure of your hostility on the road. Since we tend to underestimate our reactivity, it may help to take this with a friend or spouse.

I Anger	Possible score	30
	High	15+
	Moderate	10-14
	Low	0-9

II Impatience	Possible score	30
	High	15+
	Moderate	8-14
	Low	0-7

III Competing Possible score   30
High   10+
Moderate   5-9
Low   0-4

IV Punishing Possible score   30
High   10+
Moderate   5-9
Low   0-4

Total   Possible score   120
High   50+
Moderate   28-49
Low   0-27

Driver Stress Profile Results

Anger   _____

Impatience   _____

Competing   _____

Punishing   _____

Total   _____

3

Angry Drivers

"Anger is a short madness."
Horace

The dusk and mist made visibility poor as my friend, Frank, drove us toward the Norwalk, Connecticut YMCA for our weekly racquetball game. We were chatting amiably, when we suddenly noticed a stalled car looming dead ahead in the far right lane of a four-lane street.

Frank instinctively veered left, but braked hard when a pickup truck, already traveling there, blocked the lane change. After holding up, momentarily, Frank fell in behind the truck, and we resumed our conversation, thinking nothing of the incident.

A block later, we stopped behind the truck at a stoplight. Frank flashed his left turn indicator. We continued talking and didn't notice for several moments that the light had changed. The truck hadn't moved. It took us a few seconds to determine that the truck's driver was punishing us for having come too close to him.

There was sufficient room to turn left behind the truck, but when Frank did this, the truck's driver wheeled his vehicle sharply in an attempt to beat us around the corner. He failed and we were ahead of him. A half block later, as we slowed to turn into the YMCA, he roared past, determined to beat us to the next stoplight, which he thought was our destination.

"He's crazy," said Frank. We both assumed the truck driver having experienced his little victory, would be satisfied, but we were wrong.

As we prepared to park, we saw the driver — realizing he had failed to block us — skid to a stop. Then, with wheels spinning, he backed up to the parking lot entrance. He was seeking a personal confrontation!

Quickly, we decided to drive through the parking lot, out another exit, and across the street to the police station. The truck didn't follow.

We were justifiably alarmed. In Bridgeport the previous year another driver, angered at being cut off, followed the offending car, and shot and killed the driver.

Thirty years ago, I had my own methods of punishing "stupid" drivers. Though less extreme than the truck driver's, they were risky and inconsiderate. On one occasion, late for an eight o'clock curtain at Jacob's Pillow, a theater in Western Massachusetts, I became enraged at a slow-moving Cadillac blocking my way along the winding two-lane highway. Neither the sound of my horn nor the flash of my lights caused the fellow to pull over. Finally, I seized the opportunity afforded by a short strip of open road and recklessly passed him.

Once by him, I felt an urge to get revenge for the

"wrong" done me, and I abruptly applied my brakes, just enough to cause the alarmed Cadillac driver to slam on *his*. Then, just before impact, I gunned my motor and sped away, exalting over "teaching him a lesson!"

Even now, thirty years after "my revenge," and no longer holding the point of view of driving that I had in those days, I can feel the adrenaline rush when I recall the images and feelings of that night.

Most angry drivers don't shoot, threaten to shoot, or even carry a gun. Few actually seek a personal confrontation. But most angry drivers do punish "bad" drivers. Cursing, shouting, horn honking, obscene gestures, scowling faces and clenched fists are a common sight on our nation's highways.

Most people have a highway "war" story to tell. One third of a seventy-five-member audience I spoke to said they had encountered a hostile driver the previous week. Fifteen said that *they* had initiated the exchange. That was just in one week. Such events are guaranteed to provoke a lively discussion among any group of drivers.

How Angry Can You Get?

Driver anger is exacerbated by roads crowded with double the number of cars of twenty years ago, while road capacities increased only eleven percent. Construction projects, rush hour commuting, large tractor trailers, and accidents hamper driving and increase frustration.

But the major responsibility for driver anger lies with the driver, not the highway.

While this statement seems like an outrageous proposition to drivers inclined to become angry easily, consider for a moment the two examples mentioned above:

Frank did not hit the truck whose driver became so angry. He made an instinctive move toward the left lane when faced with the stalled car; but he did not try to force the truck to yield, and he stopped in plenty of time to let the truck pass. Understandably, the truck driver would have experienced a momentary feeling of anxiety when he thought about what might have happened if Frank had kept coming.

"Wow, that was a close call," he might have (appropriately) thought to himself afterward.

The truck driver's reaction was significantly stronger. He was enraged by an action which he considered a threat to his safety. He was out for blood! (See Table 1) On a scale from one to ten, where zero denotes complete contentment, and ten expresses the highest degree of killing rage of which we are capable, the truck driver's response had to have been at least eight. We feared it might have been ten. It was an over-reactive response to a close call, a relatively common but minor occurrence. I say over-reactive, because it is unlikely that he would have gotten much angrier even if an accident had occurred.

Consider: would the truck driver's anger been any worse if Frank had actually hit him? Would he have murdered over an accident? Suppose an accident had occurred and the truck driver had broken his leg, and was off work for six weeks. Would he have been any angrier? What if, in addition, his truck had been totaled, and he lost his job? Angrier still?

Probably not. But asking these questions puts into sharp focus what I mean when I say that the major responsibility for driver's anger lies with the driver, not the highway. In the encounter with the truck driver, circumstances justified a stress reaction on his part of three to five on the anger intensity scale. This man went up to an eight or more. His overreaction was *his* responsibility, no one else's.

TABLE 1
RANKING ANGER INTENSITY

RANK	DESCRIPTION OF MOOD
0	Perfectly relaxed, content, and peaceful.
1	Ordinary wakefulness, good mood.
2	Energetic, briskly solving problems.
3	Trying harder, extra effort, and troubled.
4	Annoyance, irritation, and increased alertness.
5	Truly aggravated, indignant, and pushing hard.
6	Just about had it, combat ready and going all out.
7	Temper flares, adrenaline surges, really mad.
8	Furious, ready to fight.
9	Rage and wrath, no holds barred.
10	Ready to kill, as angry as we can get.

In my own vendetta with the Cadillac driver, it was my responsibility for running late, not his. He had the right to travel at the speed he chose. Perhaps he felt as strong in this conviction as I did in mine. Any inclination he might have had to courteously pull off the road to let me pass could easily have been blotted out by my aggressive tailgating. Maybe he had poor vision and feared pulling over, or maybe he wanted to make the same performance I did. Many reasons could justify his behavior without making him a "bad" guy.

I overreacted to being late in the first place. By passing him I saved one minute in covering the remaining two miles. For this I risked making a dangerous pass, a possible collision, and certainly caused three other people, one in my car and two in his, to have their hearts in their throats.

The highway event triggers the reaction, but the extent of the reaction is the driver's responsibility.

WHAT *IS* STRESS?

The many ways "stress" is defined can contribute to some confusion. Most professionals like myself define it as the body's internal response to events: the outpouring of stress hormones, adrenaline, noradrenaline, and cortisol into the blood stream. Many popular publications, including, regrettably, the American Heart Association, call the external event stress. But if we use the word "stress," to mean the external event, we're left with no way to describe the internal reaction, and we need one. Medical knowledge and treatment focus on this internal reaction, not on the external event. Each individual has much more power to change the internal response than to alter the external event.

Medically speaking, therefore, by *stress,* I refer to the internal response. The word *stressor* refers to the external event.

Drivers shoulder the principal responsibility for the extent of their Stress Response, even though highway events, including other drivers, may serve as Stressors.

Many angry drivers are angry *before* they get in the car. They overreact with anger to minor frustrations: long lines at checkout counters, a pedestrian slowly walking across the street in front of them, or a spouse who forgets to do something agreed upon.

Even Saturday morning grocery shopping can be a battle for the angry driver.

"Come on slowpoke, get moving."

"Look at what she just did! Typical woman driver!"

"When are they going to fix this goddamned stop sign?"

"OK, Grandpa, we know you're brain dead!"

"That f---er is trying to steal my parking spot!"

Most of these remarks aren't heard by the "offending" driver. Nor do they see the red face, nor feel the fist slamming the steering wheel or the dashboard.

But the angry driver's passengers! Well, that's another story. It's white knuckle time. How can such a simple jaunt become such a nightmare?

Any attempt to mollify, soothe, or reason with the angry driver such as, "Calm down, what's the big deal?"; "Take it easy"; "Slow down" or "You're making me nervous" kindles self-righteous indignation and rage: "I don't have time to waste."

Challenging this argument by suggesting, "But you'll only save five minutes. Slow down so we can talk," incites further wrath.

"Shut up! If you don't like the way I drive, get out! If you want to talk, talk — I can hear you!"

To angry drivers, it is *never* a simple trip! They are truly troubled by anything that impairs their performance, or threatens to. Their pride is at stake!

While I have focused on angry drivers who are visibly angry, there are a vast number of angry drivers who don't show their anger. One of the angriest men I've treated was the sweetest, most soft-spoken man I could ever hope to meet. Inside, however, he experienced constant vigilant anger at other drivers.

Many men and women, kind and considerate face to face, will adamantly refuse to slow down for the pedestrian in the crosswalk, a vehicle attempting to ease into a crowded street from a driveway, or another driver who simply wants to change lanes. Angry drivers lose feelings of compassion for the other person. They rarely put themselves in the other's place. (How would they feel as a pedestrian with a speeding automobile bearing down on them?)

They are preoccupied with their own agenda, and feel a sense of anxiety and dread, often of phobic proportions, that something or someone will thwart them.

Something as simple as a trip to the grocery store, as minor as a close call with another vehicle, as trivial as being late for the theater, can energize this anxiety, signaling alarm and eliciting defensive anger.

Let's look more closely at this inner anxiety.

4

Understanding Your
Anger

"Through purely logical thinking we can attain no
knowledge whatsoever of the empirical world."
Einstein

Anger arises when your beliefs are challenged. If you
believe drivers should drive within the posted speed
limit, you'll become angry if someone goes faster.
If you believe that under no circumstances should anyone
cut you off, you'll become angry when that happens.

Viewed in this way, anger has a constructive purpose
in enabling human beings to create a coherent world. Anger
is the energy that alerts us to something being amiss in our
world, and it empowers us to put things back in order. If my
name is John and someone insists it is Peter, I will feel some
degree of anger and annoyance until I set the matter
straight.

We not only construct beliefs about concrete objects,
but we also construct beliefs about "rules for behavior" that

are necessary to satisfy our goals. If you conclude, for example, that "honesty is the best policy," this will serve to organize and determine your behavior when decisions about telling the truth arise. If you absolutely believe that honesty is the best policy, you will become angry with yourself when you behave in such a way that challenges that belief. For example, if a cashier gives you too much change, you will feel anger and contempt for yourself if you think "Why not keep it?"

Actually, our beliefs become increasingly complex as we go through life. "Honesty is the best policy" changes through experience as other considerations come into play. Stopped by a police officer for speeding, most individuals will not respond to his query, "Did you know how fast you were going?" by replying, "Yes, officer, I was going seventy-five, fully knowing I was breaking the fifty-five mile per hour law!"

In that situation "honesty is the best policy" will most likely not serve if you wish to avoid a ticket. As we rewrite rules for behavior, we become less angry at ourselves for events that once would have sorely vexed us. For example, as "honesty is the best policy" becomes modified by exceptions to the rule, we do not get angry at ourselves for telling the police officer, "I'm terribly sorry, Officer, I had no idea I was going so fast. I won't let it happen again."

As our understanding, awareness, and appreciation of complexity deepens, our rage lessens. The principle at work here suggests ways in which anger can be dramatically reduced when you modify your highway rules by systematically developing exceptions to them. It certainly worked for me. At one time I would easily "blow my top" when driving. Now I look forward to driving as "a port in the storm," almost never becoming even mildly annoyed. I have taught this method to scores of individuals in heart attack prevention treatment groups.

I've asked myself two questions in developing what I call the Larson Highway Stress Reduction Method:

1. What are the beliefs about driving that are being challenged by the experience of driving?
2. How can these anger-causing beliefs be modified, enlarged upon, or supplanted by other beliefs that have greater priority or serve my interests better?

FIVE DRIVERS — FIVE BELIEFS

There are five beliefs that produce highway anger when events on the road challenge drivers. The types of drivers holding these beliefs have attitudes which are readily identifiable:

1. The Speeder: Make Good Time

The Speeder believes that he should drive to his destination as fast as possible within a certain self-prescribed amount of time.

Anger results when the rate of speed or time schedule cannot be accomplished. Whoever or whatever is deemed responsible for bringing about the delay becomes the object of rage. A person making a wrong turn, a slow-moving pedestrian in a crosswalk, a stalled vehicle blocking the lane, road construction, an unexpected stop sign, a traffic jam, are events that "turn on" the Speeder.

2. The Competitor: Be Number One

The "national obsession" — The Competitor embodies the belief that the way to gain self-esteem and status is to beat the driver of another car in some self-created contest.

Anger results when the other driver appears to be

winning or actually does win the contest created in the Competitor's mind. The "contest" may be a race at high speeds, or who merges ahead of whom, or who gets through a tollbooth line first, or which lane moves faster in a traffic jam.

3. The Passive/Aggressor: Try and Make Me

The passive/aggressor believes that he loses self-esteem or status by giving in and allowing a demanding driver to have his or her way. Anger results when the other driver persists, escalates his efforts, or actually succeeds in achieving his objective. That objective may be to pass, drive faster, merge, go slow, or cut in front of the Passive/Aggressor.

4. The Narcissist: They Shouldn't Allow It

The Narcissist believes that any driver, vehicle, driving behavior, or highway activity that fails to measure up to his self-created, unrelenting standard should be banned from the road which he occupies.

The Narcissist gets angry whenever he observes an "infraction" of his standard. Common elements which conflict with the arbitrary standards may include speed, gender of driver, lane changing, make of car, automobile decorations, age of driver, attitudes of other drivers, or the consequences of highway construction.

5. The Vigilante: Teach 'em A Lesson

The driver who acts as policeman, judge and jury believes that he has the right to punish other drivers whose motoring threatens, annoys, inconveniences or fails to measure up to his self-created standards.

Anger, already present in the Vigilante, escalates when an infraction occurs and peaks as he delivers punishment. Punishment may consist of swearing, making obscene gestures, pounding on the wheel or dash, scowling, shouting obscenities, blocking another offending vehicle, running the other vehicle off the road, or even killing the other driver.

WHAT CAN WE DO?

If you recognize yourself as holding one or more of these five beliefs there is something you can do about it.

First, you must understand that most of your anger on the highway stems from these beliefs.

Second, in order to reduce your anger you need to fashion new beliefs that will compete for your attention with these old ones at the point when the provoking incident occurs.

Third, changing these five beliefs will automatically alter the context within which you perceive the provoking incident, and your attitude toward the provoking incident will also change so that you will not react as angrily.

You can better comprehend these three steps by understanding the basic way your brain processes information coming to it from your sensory receptors (eyes, ears, nose, etc.). Using the Necker cube, shown below, I'm going to demonstrate how this works:

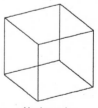

Necker cube

When you stare at it, the cube will appear to shift or flip-flop. First, one of the large squares seems closest to you, and then suddenly, the other one does. No matter how hard you try to keep one of the squares in the forefront, you can't. Moreover, the more you look at it, the faster the switching occurs. And if you make up your mind to view it only one way and then say, "I will not allow myself to look at it any other way," the image will shift before you can finish your sentence.

The reason for the shifting is that the sensory input coming through your eyes to your brain, permits two equally valid conclusions. Interestingly, the brain does not see the image as a flat two dimensional drawing of interconnecting lines (which it really is), but as a three dimensional cube. Previous data already in the brain converts the lines into a familiar object, a cube. Thus stimulated, the brain fills in the missing third dimension and that's the way it appears to us. But it cannot compute which square is closer. Each is equally possible and our perception keeps switching.

This exercise reveals an operation of the brain beyond "will power." You actually see two different conclusions; you believe two different "beliefs." You believe whatever you brain concludes at any given moment. Your will power has nothing to do with it.

This phenomenon has pivotal importance in modifying or changing the beliefs that produce highway anger. Your relationships with drivers of other cars differ from most of your other relationships in that you know very little if anything about them, except the type of car they drive. Most of the time you don't even know what the drivers look like. Your brain has to reach conclusions based on very meager data. Under these circumstances, your conclusions may be wrong, yet, as with the Necker cube, you believe you are right.

If you can conceive and believe in another, equally probable conclusion, the brain will flip over to that point of view. And, if the alternative conclusion is less stressful, you will automatically become less angry. Even if you flip back and forth like you do with the Necker cube, the time you spend viewing the incident with the less stress-producing conclusion will reduce your overall anger level.

The point may seem obvious: If you wish to be less angry on the highway, make driving more pleasant, safer and much saner, your task is to learn alternative convictions for the five stress-producing beliefs described above.

Sometimes this happens spontaneously, when you become aware of something that actually produces an alternate conclusion. A friend of mine remembered coming to a four-way stop in Westport. After stopping his car he began to cross the intersection only to find his way impeded by another car going through the stop sign to his right. He stopped to let it pass, but before he could get going again another car did the same thing and forced him to stop a third time. He became angry and rolled down his window to yell at the last driver. However, just as he yelled a profanity, he noticed yet another car closely following that one and he suddenly became aware, to his chagrin, that he had just sworn at a funeral procession.

His rage disappeared immediately. You've probably had similar experiences, and may have felt embarrassed by your misinterpretation of the data. Of course, in incidents of this type, the shift in perception comes from new data supplied by the environment. On the highway there is rarely new data to facilitate a change in perceptions so we need to supply the alternative point of view ourselves.

This is difficult to do on a case by case basis. No matter how much we try to find some redeeming quality in the person who has just cut us off, nothing helps; we remain furious. The reason for difficulty in doing it on a case by case basis is that, unlike the Necker cube, we are not aware of all the cues we are reacting to. Indeed, it may not be that being cut off, per se, is what makes us mad, rather, we believe that in the act of cutting us off the other driver has "bested" us — that's what does it.

From working with hundreds of men and women who tell me of their highway madness, I've concluded that the five beliefs already described are the key elements. Being cut off in itself does not result in rage; annoyance, perhaps, but not rage. Being bested results in rage for the "Competitor." Rather than having to come up with a special point of view for each occasion, you only have to develop alternatives for the five beliefs described, and learn how to apply them.

Take A Different Approach

Here are the five alternative beliefs, listed in the same order as the stressful ones:

1. Make Time Good replaces the *Speeder's: Make Good Time*. What is most important is to experience the joy of the journey to the maximum. You cannot see the beauty of the scenery, engage fully in a meaningful conversation with companions, feel relaxed, hear music or words, or appreciate the intimacy of others while you are preoccupied with fast driving or keeping to a tight schedule.

By allowing yourself plenty of time to drive comfortably to your destination, all the anger created by the inevitable traffic circumstances that threaten tight schedules simply disappears.

2. Number One Being replaces the *Competitor's : Be Number One.* Self-esteem is most reliably enhanced by being good to yourself, by treating yourself with all the consideration you can muster. Self-esteem generated by winning some competition is of short duration, lasting only until the next Competitor appears. The feeling of triumph is mixed with anger. Self-esteem that comes from being good to yourself, while not as heady, lasts much longer (as long as the good treatment continues). Furthermore, it serves to make you more resilient when stressful events occur, reducing the amount of anger.

Some of the ways to accomplish this are by personalizing your vehicle, keeping it clean and well maintained; giving yourself plenty of driving time to enhance the pleasure of travel; having tapes with the type of music you enjoy; being well supplied with food and drinks for those longer trips; and thinking of driving as worthwhile and pleasurable in itself (in place of viewing it as wasted time until you get to your destination).

3. Be My Guest replaces the ***Passive/Aggressor's: Try and Make Me.*** Courtesy is the essence of civilized behavior. Giving other drivers the benefit of the doubt about their motivations and treating them with the consideration with which you would like to be treated, makes for a pleasant atmosphere in your own vehicle.

An attitude of willingness to cooperate or accommodate other drivers' desires is beneficial, as long as you can do it safely, without delaying yourself, endangering others, or troubling your passengers.

4. Live and Let Live replaces the ***Narcissist's: They Shouldn't Allow Them On The Road.*** This is the belief that minding your own business and using your energy and creativity to make *your* journey interesting and enjoyable to yourself and your passengers is the best way to focus your time. Admit that you have no power to control who travels the same road. There is no entitlement — anyone can be there. Time and energy spent looking for things you don't like serve no purpose, they only pollute your vehicle with hostility.

Most people are reasonable, well-intentioned, and cooperative. Adopt an attitude that assumes this and looks upon departures from the norm much the same as, when walking along a wooded trail, you would view a rock, hole, or puddle in your path, namely, an inconvenience easily solved.

5. Leave Punishment To The Police replaces the *Vigilante's Teach 'em a Lesson.* It is rarely helpful to other drivers, yourself, and least of all to passengers, for you to assume the role of "Lord High Executioner." Moreover, it's apt to inflame the situation, putting you and others at risk of bodily harm.

Taking an attitude that most driver mishaps are not motivated by personal intention to harm, threaten, or endanger others, but by speed, miscalculation, forgetfulness, fatigue and inattention, reduces anger.

Being intellectually aware of alternative beliefs is not sufficient to accept them, for the stress-promoting beliefs are nurtured by roots going back to childhood. Before they can be supplanted by new attitudes, some of these roots need to be hacked away, and the new beliefs need to be nourished with a little friendly attention. The procedure will be painless for you, and indeed can be interesting and enjoyable. All it requires is for you to read, carefully, the next five chapters, do some simple exercises, imagine extravagant happenings, memorize new beliefs and simple poems, practice-practice-practice, and you will be amazed at how pleasurable driving will become.

5

The Speeder:
Make Good Time

"Speed, speed we are the makers of speed
Let's go. Watch our smoke. Excuse our dust."
Carl Sandburg

I vividly remember, riding with my father the thirty-six miles from our Wisconsin home to St. Paul, Minnesota. Perched on the edge of the seat, both hands on the dashboard, I felt excitement and fear as he rushed along the narrow, winding, two-lane 1930s highway.

Passing slower vehicles had to be timed to occur before reaching a hill, curve, or approaching car. Father often worked his way up through a long line of cars, passing one at a time on the short straightaways. Mindful of almost daily stories of head-on collisions under such circumstances, I was constantly preoccupied with the thought, "Will we make it?"

In those days drivers often passed on hills and curves. They took a chance. My father never was that careless, but

I can remember close calls when he just managed to get back into the proper lane before an approaching car came roaring by.

Invariably, soon after arriving at our destination, my father was asked, "How long did it take you to drive over?"

"Just under one hour."

I can still hear the response, echoed hundreds of times in the memories of my youth. "You made good time!"

It is easy to see why my father and other members of his generation came to be enormously impressed with speed; a horse walked at only four miles per hour; cars moved at least *ten times* faster. That meant the seven mile journey to town from the farm on which I was born took almost two hours by horse, while a car whizzed over the distance in less than fifteen minutes. Very impressive! As the cars went faster, travel time became even shorter. The value of "getting there fast" became etched in people's minds because the wonder and awe of moving so fast had never been experienced before in all the world's history.

I learned from my father. Unlike him, I had no experience with the horse; I just adopted his belief in the value of making good time — getting there fast. I took on the value by modeling, listening, and watching his constant articulation of that belief. Consequently, I drove fast, not pushing fifty miles per hour like my dad, but pushing seventy miles per hour.

My son, who is now twenty-six, tells me that he had the same apprehension driving with me that I had driving with my father. Once when he was ten, he wore a football helmet during a drive. It was his way of letting me know that the way I drove could result in an accident affecting his life. At the time I did not think his protective head gear was funny and I reminded him that I was a very good driver. I firmly explained to him that I got to my destination fast, without accident, or a speeding ticket. I did not think it relevant that my passengers were in fear of their lives. Getting there fast and making good time was my top priority.

As we have discussed in Chapter One, American culture reveres speed. Automobile advertisements celebrate tire-screeching acceleration; they marvel at how quickly a car goes from zero to sixty and how fast it can whip around curves and along winding roads. It is easy to understand how belief in the value of speed has become firmly affixed in those of us who live in this era of spectacular discoveries in travel and communication. But let's take a look at whether making good time is always good. *Is* faster better? Is it always true that speed of accomplishment should take priority over all other considerations?

When comparing travel time between horse and car, "going faster" has obvious advantages. However, "going faster" has exaggerated value far beyond actual the benefit when 40 mph is compared to 60 mph. The savings in time when travelling seven miles at the higher speed is merely five minutes, scarcely time enough to say hello and renew acquaintance with a friend you meet after arriving in town.

The five-minute savings in travel time costs much more in terms of enjoyment, yet, drivers take pride in shaving minutes, when "making good time" has ceased to have any real value.

Adhering to values such as "make good time" and "faster is better" is the cause of a major health problem: anger. Many drivers become angry and frustrated when something interferes with their ability to make good time. Highway obstructions and constructions imperil that goal. Traffic tie-ups make it impossible to keep it. Slow drivers seem to crop up with annoying rapidity just when the way seems to be clear. A passenger in the car who is getting hungry, or has to go to the bathroom becomes a source of annoyance, irritation and anger.

Jill, a no-nonsense, energetic, middle-aged woman is a good example of how delay can frustrate a speed-minded driver:

"I drive to our farm in Vermont every Friday night. From Westport it takes me three hours door to door. When the traffic moves right along I feel fine, although I do find myself getting tense if it begins to rain. I'm afraid we might be delayed. There can be a real traffic tie-up going through Hartford. I really get irritable then. I can't stand to be late, so when that happens I get mad all over again at those imbeciles who designed the Hartford interchanges. Once we get past Springfield I can relax. Although once I remember I missed the turnoff at Brattleboro. So stupid! I was furious with myself. Fred, my husband, kept telling me to calm down. Poor man. One time he had some type of stomach upset and had to keep stopping at practically every filling station along the road to use the restroom. I'm afraid I was not very gracious about it and we had a furious row."

Faced with a delay that made it impossible for Jill to achieve her three-hour goal, she felt anxious and apprehensive swiftly followed by being irritated and angry. When she blamed her husband Fred and his "inconsiderate" diarrhea she felt hate. In either case, the stress hormones generated contributed to the hypertension from which Jill suffered.

Ted, a soft-spoken, gracious, middle-aged director of a corporation's research and development department, left his home promptly at 7:00 A.M. for a one hour commute to his company's office. Driving as fast as the traffic would bear he sought to walk through the doorway at work just as the reception room clock turned to 8:00 A.M. On good days he arrived five minutes early; on bad days he could be five or ten minutes late. Initially, he regarded it as a game, something to add interest to a boring ride. However, it gradually became a struggle when unexpected delays occurred. He followed the same formula going home, experiencing this suspenseful contest twice daily. This adrenaline-fueled flight produced stress hormones that contributed to his two heart attacks, and ultimately I regret to say, to his death from heart failure.

Jill and Ted displayed varying degrees of time urgency, attitudes they share with many drivers. People with time urgency don't think of it as abnormal. They regard their behavior as an anxious response to excessive demands on their time.

A closer examination of this symptom is in order.

Time urgency, as a medical condition, needs to be distinguished from being in a hurry. Not all people who are in a hurry have time urgency. The ambulance driver speeding a heart attack victim to a hospital has a normal sense of time urgency. Saving time is paramount. Traffic delays could cost the life of a victim being transported.

However, to have a sense of impending disaster (like Jill) when no threat exists constitutes time urgency — the medical condition. Medical time urgency can range from mild to severe.

The *mild* variety occurs when an individual rushes to avoid being late even though the consequences of delay aren't serious. Rushing to arrive in time for the theater illustrates this. While it may be inconvenient, disappointing, and bothersome to arrive after the performance starts, any sense of impending disaster and anger are exaggerated.

Moderate time urgency is experienced by the individual who feels worried about being late even though he has adequate time. For example, airline shuttles leave from La Guardia Airport in New York to Washington, D. C. every hour. A forty-five minute drive gets you to the airport from Norwalk, Connecticut. The driver who leaves two hours prior to flight time, but instantly experiences time urgency is troubled by this condition.

Severe time urgency refers to situations like Jill's in which there is no reason for the rush at all. Whether she makes the journey in three hours, four hours, or even five hours is of no importance. She arbitrarily imposes a deadline on herself. The hurry is all internal. A "disaster" lies only in her perception that if she does not live up to her self-imposed standard of driving time she will have failed somehow as a person.

Chronically afflicted is the person who cannot sit still even three minutes to let his car warm up on a cold morning, for example, even though he has the day off and is only going to get a newspaper. Sitting in the car he feels a sense of dread in the pit of his stomach after less than thirty seconds. He guns his engine, but the anxiety grows. Finally, after a minute and a half, he starts off in order to ease his tension, his engine still coughing and sputtering.

The fact that the degree of tension experienced is more than the situation justifies makes time urgency a medical condition. This comes about through the action of stress hormones in the body. As a person hurries and continues in a state of hyperarousal and vigilance, his stress hormones gradually deplete the neurotransmitters in his brain. The brain loses the capacity to soothe itself. Biochemical depletion of brain neurotransmitters prevents the normal moderating effects of the brain's feedback circuits. As a result, the tension persists and gives rise to a sense of time urgency. Racing against time actually *creates* a feeling of not having enough time.

This state of emotional and physical fatigue cannot be helped by hurrying — the remedy Jill tried to use. Hurrying may cause a subjective symptom to disappear, as long as the driver can go faster and faster without interruption. But the underlying depletion will get more severe. On the nights Jill drove to Vermont she had such a hard time "winding down" after her trip that sleep was almost impossible.

A story is told of a driver who was stopped for speeding by a state trooper. He justified his rush by saying, "My fuel indicator is on empty. I need to get to a gas station before I run out." Of course, speeding uses up more car fuel the way rushing uses more brain fuel, ultimately creating *more* tension, not less.

The paradoxical aspect of time urgency is that in order to have the feeling of more time, a person must go slower, not faster. It seems counterintuitive, but it is true. By giving up dedication to speed, you can relax, recharge your neuroreceptors, and consequently, drive more slowly with less tension. Less tension means reduction in time urgency, and reduction in time urgency means that you feel there is more time.

Speed has another drawback. The faster you go, the narrower your range of sensory experience. The faster you go, the less you can attend to conversations, music, or scenery, for example. Life becomes more narrow. Sensory contact with your immediate surroundings is diminished.

You can experiment with this by taking a walk in a beautiful area. Start out walking at a fast rate of speed, then stop completely. Notice how much more you can see, hear and smell when you stand still than when you were walking. Begin walking again and notice that is impossible to attend fully to the sensory input from your environment.

In physics there is a law called the Heisenberg Uncertainty Principle, which states that you cannot know accurately both the location and the speed of a particle. The better you know the location, the less you can know the speed, and vice versa. The same is true with driving. Call it the Highway Uncertainty Principle: the more you speed the less you experience where you are. The more you experience where you are the slower you go. Speeding, though it gets you to the goal quickly, robs you of the richness of life's experiences. Standing still, though it optimizes the richness of sensory experiences, doesn't get you to your destination. You can only maximize one at a time, you can't have both. Which do you choose? It seems reasonable to choose to drive at a rate that allows you to optimize the journey's enjoyment within a reasonable time.

This shift in priorities can best be expressed as: *Make Good Time / Make Time Good.*

POSITIVE STEPS FOR THE SPEEDER

In order to have *make time good* become an automatic value that you live by, you must endow it with greater importance. There are a number of ways to accomplish this. First, clarify your goals by answering the following questions:

- Do you want to enjoy your companions and make their journey more pleasurable?
- Do you want to experience the beauty of the scenery?
- Do you want your children to be better behaved?
- Do you want to enjoy music or other tapes more?

- Do you want to savor the taste of food and beverages?
- Do you want to really enjoy yourself?

If you answer yes to these questions, you are ready for the big step. The next time you drive, figure the approximate driving time it usually takes and allow an extra fifty percent. If the journey ordinarily takes an hour, allow an hour and a half. I do this routinely when I drive into New York City for the theater. To arrive for an eight o'clock curtain, I leave at half past six. Going to church on Sunday morning, where the driving time is twenty minutes, I leave thirty minutes before the service.

If you are a typical Speeder, this will not come easily. Leaving with so much extra time may bring apprehension. You may think arriving early will be a "waste of time." For the fast driver nothing is so repugnant as getting to the destination with "time to spare." Like Ted, whose goal was to arrive precisely "on time," getting there "ahead of time" is experienced as a failure. The individual feels anxious and doesn't know what to do with the extra time. When speeding, you lose the capacity to enjoy extra time. Nothing seems important except to get there.

You can eradicate this apprehension by trying the extra time allotment experiment three times. I guarantee that after arriving with time to spare, you will find ways to make extra time worthwhile and pleasurable. But you have to experience it in order to believe it. You will find that the extra time goes by quickly, and results in added enjoyment.

I remember the first occasion on which I decided to drive a long distance at a 50 to 60 MPH speed, rather than my usual 70 to 75 MPH. My wife and I had just spent a weekend in the Catskills, and we started the three-hour drive home. I decided to take my time, enjoy the beautiful fall colors and share my thoughts with my wife. We had a marvelous trip together. At the slower speed I could concentrate on what she had to say. Since we were not in a rush, we stopped at several interesting spots which we would not have noticed at a faster speed. Moreover, paradoxically, the time flew by, even though the actual travel time was thirty minutes longer. Since that time in 1985, I usually plan my automobile journeys so I can drive at a leisurely rate.

By changing your overriding attitude toward time, a host of highway events stop being stressors, including:

- Travel time
- Slow drivers who slow your speed
- Delays due to construction or accidents
- Delays due to weather
- Unplanned stops to eat or use the toilet

To facilitate this change in beliefs, I suggest that you use a three-by-five card to list your old and new beliefs.

On one side write:

Old Beliefs

Stressor: Driving to destination

Make good time

Drive as fast as possible

Get out of my way

Break a new record

Faster is better

On the other side write:

New Beliefs

Event: Driving to destination

Make time good

I may not pass this way again

Enjoy my companion

Quality not quantity

Enjoy sounds, sights, smells

Use your own wording and put down the personal values that mean the most to you. *Carry the card with you when you drive,* and review it before starting out. Memorize both sides of the card, so that you know what you've written by heart. Read it before bedtime. You will create an alternative attitude to take along every time you start out towards some destination. As with the Necker cube, once your mind grasps another way to interpret the stimulus (driving to destination), the new attitude will kick in automatically, and you'll soon drive in a more leisurely manner.

Another technique may also aid you. When I was a kid, Burma Shave signs dotted the nation's highways. These small signs, about six to eight in number, were posted along the edge of the road and each sign continued a clever limerick. Sponsored by a shaving cream company, the signs were enjoyable and broke up the monotony of a long drive. Here is my nomination for a new series of Burma Shave-type signs about speeding:

Rushing along
Is just fine,
If you don't mind
A coffin of pine.
But a gentle passage
Brings a better view,
And would be my choice,
How about you?

Make time good.

6

The Competitor:
Be Number One

"Who's going to be first?"

American teachers

The inclination to create private competitions while driving was taken to new heights by Bill, a ruddy-faced, graying Manhattan executive, who made his daily commute into New York City an "Olympic Games" event.

Event 1: He rushed to complete his morning exercises, shower and breakfast, striving to leave precisely at 7:00 A.M.

Event 2: At 7:00 A.M. he started his engine and raced off to his office, aiming to walk in just as the clock reached 8:00 A.M.

Event 3: Landmarks along the route — tollbooths, the New York state line, first glimpse of the Manhattan skyline, and so on, served as checkpoints. Did he pass them on time, early or late?

Event 4: He'd pick out another high-powered car and

race against it to some marker he'd selected — a tollbooth or highway exit.

Event 5: At tollbooths, he'd choose cars waiting in another lane, and compete to see who paid the toll first.

Event 6: At coin-operated automatic toll stations he'd toss his coin in the basket, then quickly accelerate, trying to pass the light *before* it turned green.

Event 7: When first in line at intersections, the green light signaled a sprint to beat the car in an adjoining lane to the other side.

Event 8: During multi-lane traffic jams, a certain vehicle in the next crowded lane became his "competition." Who would move ahead faster?

Event 9: Another car, traveling more slowly and blocking his path in the left lane, became a personal challenge. How fast could he devise a way to pass it?

Event 10: His "dislike" for certain cars sparked a moral competition in which he bested them by getting ahead and staying there.

These competitions were fun to Bill only if he won easily. If he began to lose, he felt annoyed, and intensified his efforts. Further losses caused his blood to boil. The fun was gone. It became a battle "to the death."

Two complications seriously escalated his aggravation: If another driver actually joined in the competition and tried to beat him, Bill became reckless, drove much too fast and made sudden lane changes.

If a particularly slow driver impeded Bill, causing him to "lose," he became furious, pounding his steering wheel and cursing.

During one of his competitions, Bill had his only accident. While keeping his eye on his competitor in a slow moving traffic jam, he struck a stopped car just ahead of him.

Bill paid his biggest price internally. He had a heart attack, secondary to the stress hormones generated by the relentless aggravation he created.

For Bill, driving became more than simply a way to get from one place to another. It became a private referendum on his self-worth. When he "won" he felt good about himself. When he "lost" he felt bad — depressed, isolated and estranged. When Bill was growing up, his parents and teachers praised him for winning competitions and punished him harshly for losing. Eventually, these attitudes became a part of Bill's thinking and remained powerful psychological reactions long after he left his parents and teachers. When he won, he inwardly praised himself and felt good; when he lost, he inwardly trashed himself and felt lousy.

From the time we are children, people are continually saying to us, "Who's going to be first?" You can find examples of such early teaching all around you. One morning while I was out walking, a young woman riding a bicycle passed me, followed in a few moments by a man on a bicycle with a child of about three seated behind him. As he rode past, I heard him say to his child, "Let's see if we can beat Mommy."

Parents, educators, and sports figures reiterate that Number One is *better* than Number Two. While parents in other cultures admonish their children to "be wise" or "be cooperative," our mentors in the United States teach us to constantly appraise our behavior in a hierarchical order from first to last.

This leads to a habit of ranking events, friends, children, athletic teams, places of residence, clothes and cars from best to worst, first to last, biggest to smallest, most to least and somebody to nobody. It leads, as with Bill, to an obsessive striving to be Number One, and a desperate concern lest we slip and lose our personal ranking.

Individuals trapped in this mode of thinking suffer multiple daily mood swings when they compare their status to that of whomever they meet or see, and perceive that someone else has it "better." Each day rings in a series of personal competitions that are either "won" or "lost."

Motorists who take this attitude with them on the road experience much greater internal stress than drivers free of this obsession. To be competitive you must be *ready, vigilant,* on your *mark* and primed to *fight.* Stress hormones stay high for the entire journey, gradually exhausting your body's endocrine glands and creating abnormally high levels of cholesterol. Over years, the presence of this internal physiologic state causes heart attacks, diabetes, hypertension and strokes.

It also increases the likelihood of accidents, since drivers intent on competing will either be:

- Distracted, and, like Bill, not looking where they're going; or,
- Reckless, and in their desire to win, will impulsively take foolish chances.

Fifteen years ago, while I was driving home from a restaurant with a date and my two children, I became impatient and perturbed by a slow-moving vehicle ahead of me. At a stoplight, I seized an opportunity and pulled into the right lane alongside the other car. At this particular intersection, the four lanes abruptly merged into two in order to go through a tunnel under a railroad overpass.

The instant the light turned green, I shot ahead and beat my opponent to the single lane passage. I won — almost. The teenage driver of the other car rose to my challenge and gunned his car; but since I was a bit ahead of him, he was forced into the left lane where he met oncoming traffic. To avoid a head-on collision, he turned sharply right, and his right front fender struck my left rear fender, sending my car careening into the left lane where I narrowly missed the oncoming vehicle.

Luckily, no one was injured. However, a short time after the incident, my date broke off our relationship. Smart lady. During that highly stressful time in my life, I not only had a slight hypertension, but three minor motor vehicle accidents in three years, plus two tickets for speeding.

American culture enshrines competition as a value not to be questioned. Our capitalist economy is based on competition. We give the highest rewards to those who have competed to be the best in athletics, movies, literature, science, academics and public achievements.

Why shouldn't drivers who compete feel positively ennobled? They are engaged in an enterprise as essential as breathing. Yet, I advocate giving up competing while driving.

The most common resistance to this idea is the fear that stopping competitive thinking on the road will lead to a general indifference to outcome. One corporation withdrew their invitation for me to speak to their employees because of this concern.

Originally, they invited me to speak because employees were arriving at work "all stressed out" from rush hour commuting. The managers wanted me to help employees calm down so they could more quickly concentrate on their jobs. The business was also losing employees as a direct result of the commuting hassles.

Arrangements for the talk went well until the two executives representing the company learned that I believed preoccupation with competition should be curtailed on the road. Both men blanched and expressed their fear that employees might also lose their desire to compete with the Japanese. They said "Sayonara" to me and cancelled the talk.

Their fear was groundless, but worthy of a fuller explanation since so many individuals harbor the same misconception. Making a better product entails a completely different mindset than that of the driver competing on the road on the way to work. The first is volitional and can be easily turned on or off. The second is an over-reactive reflex; the driver who competes cannot simply decide to stop it (as explained earlier). If it were easy, I wouldn't need to write this book.

Making a better product is achieved through teamwork, while competing on the road is a cutthroat activity. Businesses run on the latter model, in which workers vie with each other, do not produce as good a product as do businesses run on the collaborative model. Experimental research confirming this dates back to the 1930s. W. Edwards Deming, an American, persuaded the Japanese to use a teamwork, quality-based model after World War II. Japanese car makers began to compete successfully against U.S. companies, and, in certain areas have dominated the market.

Finally, making a better product requires concentration. The act of competing on the road produces distraction and a decreased ability to concentrate. That's what brought the two executives to my office in the first place. I could have aided their workers in developing the mindset that would decrease their stress and increase their ability to concentrate, and have a greater sense of affiliation with each other. It is almost certain that this would have resulted in their turning out a superior product, better than the one they're producing now.

The same fear of decreasing competition was expressed by the Pentagon when the Friedman Institute proposed teaching stress-reduction attitudes to U.S. Army colonels attending the U.S. Army War College. While Pentagon officials recognized the need for stress reduction to lower the heart attack rate among its officers, they were concerned that leadership quality and ability might decline. Consequently, a rigorous research protocol measuring the fate of all attributes of leadership was followed. Any decline in leadership ability would be reason to immediately terminate the stress-reduction program.

The findings, published in the *American Heart Journal* in 1985, revealed that in *every dimension measured* the officers became better leaders, not worse. The Friedman protocol for stress reduction continues to be part of the War College's curriculum.

Similarly, I have no doubt that you'll become better, more efficient Competitors where it counts, by being less competitive on the highway where it's inappropriate.

You, the man on the bicycle, Bill and I have knowledge of the alternative, but we do not realize we are making a choice that excludes it. Human consciousness is limited at any moment by what we're paying attention to. If we're intent on winning a race, we will not be able to take in the scenery along the route. If we become transfixed by the beauty of the scenery, we will not reach the finish line.

We live our lives along this continuum of choice. As the following diagram illustrates, at one extreme (1) is the fixed *intention-attention* to strive and compete to reach some goal. At the other extreme (2) is the fixed *intention-attention* to fully experience the joy of being alive. It's impossible to have it both ways.

The shaded portions of the diagram represent the hormones associated with each intention-attention. Goal directedness requires adrenaline and noradrenaline. Experiencing the pleasure of being alive requires endorphins. Most of life is a blend of these hormones plus cortisol, which accompanies all stimulation.

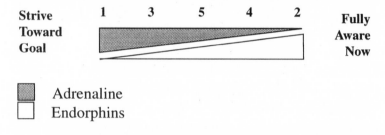

Individuals with the intention-attention to be Number One spend too much time near Number Three on the chart resulting in an increased likelihood of stress illnesses and accidents and a decreased enjoyment of life. The flower children of the 1960s spent too much time near Number Four on the chart, resulting in isolation, aimlessness, boredom, and drug use.

You can live your life at Number Five. You can accomplish goals and enjoy life. Shifts can be made in either direction depending on what you determine is in your best interest at any one time.

How does this apply to the road? The following illustrations will help us to understand. They are taken from different capacities of experiencing: sight and sound.

First, take sight. We see, but the quality of our seeing and our ability to enjoy what we see can vary dramatically. There are at least four levels of quality:

1. Unconscious Seeing: We see, but we're not aware of it. While driving we may miss our exit, or realize that we've passed a familiar landmark without taking notice of it. We're not aware of any particular feeling.

2. Black-White Seeing: We see, but we're not aware of color; objects appear in tones of gray. We feel interest and curiosity.

3. Postcard Color Seeing: We see in color, but objects are not fully three dimensional. We feel interest and curiosity plus joy and pleasure in the beauty.

4. Two And One-Half Dimensional Seeing: Probably the way we see things when we're rested; we see color, and some sense of depth. We feel happy and admire beauty.

5. Three Dimensional Seeing: We see in color, and we are keenly aware of the space between a near object and one farther away. We feel a thrill at being alive; we're aware of a supreme sense of awe.

When we speak of improving the quality of our lives, we would all agree that being able to see vivid color is better than being limited to black and white. Given a choice, most of us would rather spend our existence at level four than at level one or two. But when we are preoccupied with competition, we are simply not aware of color's magnificence.

The same considerations apply to hearing. Hearing quality varies enormously. As with any radio or sound system, adjustments can be made for volume, tone, clarity, treble, bass, rhythm, texture and color. The quality of our hearing can range along the following dimensions:

1. Sound Without Words: We hear a noise, but cannot distinguish a voice.
2 . Low Impact Words: We hear, but the words register faintly, as if from far away. A child may tug at our clothes to get our attention. We may feel annoyed when our preoccupation is interrupted.
3. Clear Words: We hear words clearly and react to their content, but the range of what we take in is blunted by our efforts to concentrate.
4. Musical Hearing: We hear the words and the melody and can take pleasure in the sound. We respond emotionally, feel empathy, and reverberate with associations.
5. Sensational Hearing: We hear and our whole bodies are aroused. We experience the sound as a physical sensation. Our spines may tingle, feet want to move and hearts and voices want to sing or shout.

We are capable of similar levels of sensation with our other capacities of experiencing. When scientists speak of us as normally using only ten percent of our brain capacity, they are referring to underdeveloped potentiality. Developing our potential for enjoyment is the opportunity present to us anytime we set off in our automobiles.

You can develop your potential to become a fully realized human being, a state I refer to as a Number One Being. As with improving seeing and hearing, developing an expanded self goes hand in hand with the growth of aesthetic sensibilities. The power of this emphasis on treating yourself as a Number One Being can be illustrated by my journey to a car wash. You may have had a similar experience, but did not appreciate its full significance. I call my experience "Car wash magic."

Before going on a spring vacation, I get everything in order: I pay my bills, bring my business up to date, clean my desk, and last, but not least, I wash my car. That way, it's waiting to welcome me when I get back.

My car — grimy from a month of winter's salt and dirt; full of papers, some important, some trash, tossed here and there in the back seat; and with a film of dust layering the windows and dashboard — causes me to feel ashamed for the neglect I display so publicly.

At the car wash, I hastily clear out the back seat and watch as the sand-filled floors are vacuumed. Next, I watch with pleasure as my car, pulled along the conveyor, gets soaped, scrubbed, and washed, before emerging.

Four men swarm over, around and through my car, rubbing, wiping, dusting, spraying and drying, earning my gratitude and tip. I begin to feel a sense of pride and joy as I slip behind the wheel.

Pulling out into the street, I notice a wonderful melodic, rhythmical hum to the engine that wasn't there when I drove in. I also marvel at the marked increase in the ease of turning the wheel and the smoothness of handling. Had they greased it, changed the oil and tuned it unbeknownst to me, somewhere along that conveyor?

The day seems brighter, too. I see clearly through my sparkling windows, and admire the smart gray hood and its graceful lines. The ride is exceptional, better than I remember it being just fifteen minutes before, and the stylish dashboard and soft leather seats delight my senses of sight and smell. Is this the same car I drove in with, or has mine been magically returned to its "new car" state?

Even more amazingly, I feel calmer and more patient. I drive with greater confidence. Moreover, the traffic flows in a more orderly fashion. As I wait for cars to clear, so I can make a left turn, I notice how courteous other drivers have become!

What in the world had happened in that car wash?

The answer is simple, yet profound: My mood had changed.

That's an endorphin high!

What makes the car wash experience so amazing and illuminating is the short time (about fifteen minutes) it takes for such a dramatic shift in perception to occur. Moreover, nothing was done directly to me, the driver. I merely saw something happen, and that was enough to markedly alter how I perceived reality. The world didn't change, *I* did.

In fifteen minutes I became less irritable and less stressed. The car wash experience suggested that if I could find a way to change my mood, I could change the way events affect me.

My change in mood at the car wash happened without conscious effort on my part. That distinguishes the endorphin high from the adrenaline high. Adrenaline highs require concentrated effort to win; endorphin highs require a mindful openness to experience sensation (as I illustrated with seeing and hearing). But you can make a conscious effort to give yourself experiences that enrich your life and improve your self-esteem in other ways than competing when you drive. Instead of trying to win competitions, you can treat yourself royally as a Number One Being. Here are some suggestions for enhancing your driving experience in positive ways:

- Drive to maximize sensory awareness. Remember the Highway Uncertainty principle I wrote about earlier: The more you speed, the less you experience where you are; the more you experience where you are, the slower you go. Find the optimum speed that allows you to reach your objective without sacrificing sensation.

- Treat yourself to beautiful and/or stimulating sounds. Key in the radio stations, take advantage of the varied subjects available on tape, from Garrison Keillor to poetry.
- Experience the fun of driving with companions. I particularly enjoy setting off on a one or two-hour journey with my wife or a good friend. Nothing will interrupt us from enjoying the sights or our conversation. If I race or compete I cannot fully attend to the conversation, or experience the pleasure and affection I feel as the dialogue ranges through many moods and ideas.
- Stock some tasty goodies in the car, such as gum or candy. Most cars have trays for drinks. Sipping a cup of coffee invites a more leisurely ambiance, and the taste sensation causes you to be more aware of other sensations, too, like hearing, seeing and smelling. Your mind moves away from preoccupation with competing, towards appreciation of the immediate benefits of being alive.
- Keep a cassette recorder near you. When you drive with this new attitude, new ideas frequently will pop into your head. Your creative mind churns them out, and if not recorded they may fade.

By shifting your attention from competing to relishing and improving the quality of your life, you are practicing "driving yourself healthy." You will increase your self-esteem, not through "earning it" by winning some made-up competition, but through experiencing a feeling of well-being by attending to those activities that make life a pleasure.

Instead of an automobile ride adding to the storm of your life, make it a *port* in the storm, a haven you can return to for replenishment.

As I wrote earlier, to facilitate this change, use a three-by-five card. On one side write:

Old Belief

Stressor: Other speeding cars

Urge: Urge to compete

                Be Number One

                Who's going to be first?

                Winning is everything

                Beat the other guy

                May the best person win

On the other side, write:

New Belief

Event: Other speeding cars

Urge: Urge to enjoy life

                Highways are too dangerous for games

                It's not worth dying for

                Number One Being: Create quality in my life

                Maximize my pleasure

                Drive myself healthy

Carry this card with you while driving and review it every day for a month before starting off. Better yet, memorize the New Belief side. It's not hard and it won't take you long.

Once committed to memory, the new beliefs will automatically and immediately modify your attitude every time you feel the urge to compete. Within one to three months of memorization, your attitude will have changed without any further effort on your part.

Finally, while you're in the memorizing mode, remember this "Burma Shave" jingle:

> Being Number One
> Can be fun.
> Getting the checkered flag
> Can be a gag,
> But a highway race
> Will cause your erase;
> The flag you'll earn
> Will be on your urn.
> Wait your turn.

Better yet, have someone else threaten to recite this jingle whenever you begin to compete!

7

The Passive-Aggressor:
Try and Make Me

"Is it worth dying for?" Eliott
"I'm thinking, I'm thinking." Jack Benny

D riving on M4, an English six-lane motorway, differs
from driving on United States interstates. English
drivers are courteous, and they quickly yield the
right of way to faster vehicles. Just a flash of the lights, and
the slower vehicle moves to the next lane at the first opportunity.

Moreover, the lane change happens readily. The driver
who must change his or her lane encounters no opposition
from cars in the middle lane. As soon as the rear directional
signal goes on, any car traveling there slows to accommodate the move. That's courtesy!

Contrast that with the "try and make me" attitude
frequently encountered on American roads. Many U.S.
motorists take it as a personal affront when a faster vehicle
seeks to pass. Even when the middle lane is open, drivers

are often reluctant to yield the right of way.

Similar attitudes make lane changes difficult, even when a motorist signals in a clear and timely manner with appropriate directional lights. As a result, U.S. drivers often play "chicken." The driver who wants to change lanes or merge with another lane simply begins the process, forcing the driver of another car to choose between certain collision or backing off.

"Here I come, ready or not. I'll hit you unless you yield!"

Such behavior results in harrowing close calls, enraged drivers, accidents, injuries, deaths and even murders.

Of the 187 incidents investigated in the summer of 1987 in Los Angeles where firearms were brandished either to threaten or to fire at other motorists, two-thirds involved circumstances in which cars were passing, merging or entering the highway. One driver had resisted yielding the right of way to another, and tempers escalated to murderous proportions! Let me introduce you to a couple of drivers who could have become statistics.

Roy, a wiry, curly-headed advertising executive, reminds me of Woody Allen. Small, intense and bursting with energy; on weekends he plays saxophone with a band that is in great demand to entertain at weddings, graduation parties and other festive occasions. However, unlike Woody Allen, Roy does not have much of a sense of humor.

At my heart attack prevention group one evening, Roy was visibly shaken and chagrined when he told us, "I lost yesterday. Someone forced me to let him pass. He got the better of me!"

While driving in the left lane of Interstate 95, Roy glanced in his mirror, noticing a sports car rapidly approaching. The driver charged up close to Roy, tailgated him and tried to edge him over. Roy felt challenged by the nudging, got himself into a contest of wills and refused to yield the right of way. (Besides, the middle lane was crowded, and Roy would have to slow down to move over.)

Mostly, however, Roy could not bear the thought of "losing" to the other driver, whom Roy was beginning to hate. He disliked the other driver's pushiness, and he believed that giving in would be acknowledging the other driver's superiority. He became intransigent.

"Make me," he said under his breath.

Then, abruptly, the other driver seized an opening, moved into the middle lane and accelerated alongside of Roy. Both men exchanged challenging glances. When the other driver gained a half-car length on Roy, he began a game of "chicken" by accelerating even more and edging over into Roy's lane, determined to insinuate himself into the five feet between Roy and the car just ahead.

Roy had to choose. Accelerating to close off the gap or even holding his own meant a collision, unless the sports car was bluffing! Accelerating also would bring him dangerously close to the car ahead of him. Roy hesitated.

When he hesitated, the sports car moved in determinedly. In another instant the cars would touch, and Roy decided to "give up." He slowed down and let the sports car pass.

As he told his story, Roy's embarrassment, humiliation and chagrin was palpable to everyone in the room. He believed he had lost. He looked down, refusing to meet anyone's eyes.

Members of the group praised him for the wisdom he had demonstrated in not risking his life so foolishly. Roy argued with us. He believed that if he had "had the guts," *he* would have accelerated and forced the sports car driver to choose between hitting *him* or backing off.

Something very powerful inside Roy brought him to the brink of risking death. If he hadn't backed off we could have said he reached ten on the anger intensity scale: *ready to die for his beliefs.* It's clear Roy overreacted to a relatively trivial happening. Of all the causes one might conceivably die for, avoiding being passed on the highway comes near the bottom of the list.

Roy now agrees that he overreacted but that night in group at Norwalk Hospital, he felt justified in his anger and was troubled that he hadn't reached a ten, and had "had the guts" to risk his life.

Passive-Aggressors like Roy aren't bad or stupid. Like the Competitor, they experience certain highway events as "win-lose" situations. Once they define the incident in those terms, they've put their self-esteem on the line. Consequently, if they "lose," they feel simply terrible, devastatingly depressed, humiliated and disgraced.

One person I knew who always "had the guts" to risk an accident was Peter. He repeatedly got into confrontations when lanes merged, but only under specific circumstances. He did not have trouble with cars merging from an entrance ramp or where two roads come together to form one — he took turns with other vehicles.

However, on a multi-lane expressway, when drivers were warned that a lane was closed for construction about a mile ahead, Peter's passive-aggressive nature came out. Seeing the warning, Peter immediately moved to the right lane, only to watch in fury as car after car passed him, traveling in the left lane. Those drivers stayed in the left lane until the last fifty yards or so before the narrowing, knowing that traffic moved faster there than in the right lane.

Peter became outraged. If he had had his way, everyone would have moved to the right lane at the warning sign. He tried to enforce this belief by driving practically bumper to bumper with the car immediately in front of him, refusing to allow anyone from the left lane to cut in after the warning sign. He had angry confrontations with aggressive drivers, especially right at the narrowing, where cars merging from the two lanes took turns. Not Peter! He battled with drivers who tried to merge. The highest stress reaction in his life came when another car successfully "bested" him.

Peter's fury knew no bounds. But part of his anger was directed at himself, for *letting it happen*. He replayed the incident over and over again in his mind, berating both himself and the "transgressor" in the other car. He had allowed too big a gap between himself and the car in front; he hadn't accelerated fast enough; he had been distracted by his wife's talk. Peter could always point to a "mistake" he had made that permitted the other car to cut him off.

To understand Peter, you would have to know about his "martinet" father. Peter was brought up to obey the family's rules. There was a right way to do things and only a right way to do things. He had to shoulder his responsibilities, excel academically, and, above all, he could not make mistakes! When he did, his father blasted him verbally, and gave him a look of withering scorn.

This made an indelible impression. So much so that when I knew Peter, who was sixty-five and ready to retire after a successful business career, he continued to lament the fact that with all his life experience, he still made "mistakes!"

What kinds of mistakes? You name it: forgetting his keys, getting lost, arriving late for an appointment, misreading directions, failing to make a promised call, or

allowing someone to cut in front of him on the highway —
all the unavoidable things that everyone does occasionally.
But for Peter there were no excuses.

Paradoxically, the pressure got worse as he got older.
Whereas most individuals become more forgiving of themselves and others with experience, Peter did not. He
believed that one should make fewer mistakes the older one
got. Thus, even the forgetfulness associated with aging,
which Peter experienced more and more often, became a
reason for scornful self-reproach.

Peter could not accept the idea that with growth and
maturation, old "truths," knowledge and assumptions often
changed becoming "wrong" or "mistaken." He couldn't
forgive himself for falling short in his own estimation.

With help from the group, Peter eventually was able to
redefine his attitude toward "mistakes." Above all, he came
to realize that his father was not always right. He had made
mistakes, too. This new understanding helped Peter become
more forgiving of himself. It also helped him to realize that
depending upon which belief he gave priority to, whenever
he made choices, he couldn't help making mistakes.

On the highway, when a warning sign says a lane is
closed one mile ahead, quickly complying with the warning
(and for Peter this was the "right" thing to do) means you
are going to go slower. If your priority lies with following
directions, you're right. If your priority lies with going
faster, you're mistaken.

It is particularly "American" to think that driving any
way we want to is our "right." Unlike the Europeans, who
long ago had to accommodate personal preference to the
idiosyncrasies of others, we still strive for "rugged individ-
ualism." Public mores, courtesy and etiquette are weak
constraints on the very personal attitudes we take to the

highway. Traveling by road is not simply a trip; with the Passive/Aggressor it's a contest of wills.

I've been on both sides of this situation. Early in my life I sought to pass other cars. Then I went through a period when I tried to obstruct Speeders from passing. Now, I have more important things to consider than trying to regulate how fast someone else should drive. My alternative to "try and make me," and viewing other drivers' aggressiveness as a personal challenge, is to treat motorists with the courtesy I would show a visitor in my home. Let "be my guest" be your new attitude, too.

"You want to pass me? Be my guest."

"You want to merge? Be my guest."

Assume the person wishing to pass is much like yourself when you've been in a hurry and wanted to pass someone else (or make a lane change). Think, "There is probably a good reason he is hurrying, I've been in his shoes myself." Make it easy for him to go on his way. Regard other drivers as people you're showing around your home, not as opposing gladiators in the Roman Coliseum. Take charge, roll out the red carpet and be courteous.

Again, this changed attitude can be facilitated by practice with three-by-five cards. On one side write:

Old Belief

Stressor: Car trying to pass or merge

Urge: Don't let 'em

Try and make me

I won't let them beat me

I don't like them

I have a right to be there

They won't push me around

On the other side write alternate attitudes, repeat them to yourself before starting off, and memorize them so that the new attitudes will affect your responses automatically. For example:

New Belief

Event: Car trying to pass or merge
Urge: Act as if the driver is a guest in
                your home
           He probably has a good reason to
                hurry
           Be my guest
           He's human, like me
           I've been in his shoes
           Make it easy for him

The first few times you practice this, you may feel uncomfortable and a little frustrated after pulling over. New thoughts might occur to you, such as, "I'm being a wimp." Or you may worry that "giving in," as Roy looked at it, will lead to your becoming a spineless patsy in other areas of your life.

If you think this way it probably means you are still investing your simple act of courtesy with the emotions of your former attitude.

Remind yourself of your new attitude by repeating the new beliefs to yourself. As you repeat them, you will notice that your frustration will abate. Every time you feel uncertain about your new decision, repeat them again. Within a month, courtesy will come easily to you.

When you stop using energy wastefully on the

highway, you will find you have more energy for assertiveness where it counts.

Here's my "Burma Shave" jingle for the Passive-Aggressor:

> I have the right of way, says she,
> I have the right of way, says he,
> I won't give in, says she,
> I won't give in, says he,
> What fools these mortals be,
> Rest in peace, say we.

8

The Narcissist: They Shouldn't Allow It

"The remedy for wrongs is to forget them."
Cyrus

Drivers commonly have a pet peeve — a highway stressor that's particularly irksome to them. With a little prodding, usually very little, they will tell you the latest war story involving other drivers' galling behavior. Here are some examples:

- Absent-minded or inconsiderate drivers who almost caused accidents
- Drivers who refused to yield the right-of-way
- Drivers who stopped inappropriately and held up traffic while trying to make up their minds
- Reckless drivers who wove in and out from lane to lane
- Highway construction that blocked lanes and caused jams

These events are recounted with enormous self-righteous fervor. A telltale phrase indicating you are hearing a pet peeve is the declaration, "They shouldn't allow those a-- h---s on the road!"

This expression describes the profound visceral rage experienced by offended drivers. The statement is not logical or calculated, the speakers are simply deeply provoked. They want to blot out, forever, the stimulus arousing their rage. *They just want the other driver to go away!* Most people who drive long enough will witness careless driving behavior as described in the five examples above, but most of us won't react with rage. For the type of driver I call the Narcissist, however, thoughtless drivers provoke a sense of personal injury and affront. The term "Narcissist" is not meant to belittle, but to explain how the extent of the Narcissist's rage derives from the set of emotional triggers with which he views improper driving.

Five characteristics are identifiable in the Narcissist.

First, two Narcissists traveling the same road will consistently report seeing quite different infractions. Jay and Peter, two members of a highway stress reduction group, frequently compare notes.

When not bristling with rage, Jay has a bumptious quality. A young Santa Claus in spirit, he can delight children at Christmas when he dons a beard and passes out gifts. Peter, whom you met, earlier, and who is about twenty-five years Jay's senior and ready to retire after a successful business career, laments the fact that despite all his life experience, he still makes "mistakes."

Jay can't abide slow drivers in the left lane of I-95 — a three-lane interstate flowing through Fairfield County, Connecticut — who refuse to pull over to let him pass. Peter, traveling the same road at approximately the same speed as Jay, seldom notices such incidents, but becomes livid recounting the number of drivers who cut him off. Jay, on the other hand, regards these happenings as routine; just part of the highway scene.

Second, the Narcissist invariably sees an example of his particular pet peeve each time he drives.

Jay can't get over it: the repetition of thoughtless, obstructionist driving alarms him every time he wants to get some place in a hurry.

"I have a right to be angry," he says. "They're usually driving a beige or pale green, old model Ford, Chevrolet, or Plymouth, and going about forty miles-per-hour in the left lane of I-95. They will not pull over! I swear, the drivers are retarded men or women. No matter how much I flash my lights or honk, they keep going their merry way. Monday I was late because one had me blocked in for five miles. I rode his ass with my high beams, the son of a bitch. Now you mean to tell me I shouldn't be mad at that f---er?"

Mike, a burly middle-aged executive, tells a more amusing and self-revealing story about the same phenom-enon. Each day on the way to the railroad station for his commute into New York, he used to drop off his son, Donny, at grade school. Mike didn't allow much time to do this, and he was forever cursing and swearing at drivers who impeded his dash to the train station. In the afternoon, the task of picking up Donny and bringing him back home fell to Mike's wife.

One day after several months of this, Donny said to his father, "Gee Dad, you ought to pick me up in the afternoon. All the a-- h---s have gone home."

A third characteristic of the Narcissist is that he believes he "knows" the personality characteristics of the offending driver, even though he has never been introduced to the driver who offended him and wouldn't be able to pick the person out in a crowd. Nonetheless, he has a sense of certainty about the kind of individual he or she must be.

George, a business executive, has a reputation among his staff for being a son of a bitch, ruthlessly pushing both himself and those who report to him. George's pet peeve is drivers who seem bewildered or indecisive. They may slow down to make a turn or to identify a street name or building address, but they hesitate to commit themselves, temporarily holding up traffic. George feels no compassion for such "inadequacy." They are all "fools who shouldn't be allowed on the road."

If Albert Einstein had lost his way and slowed, uncertain of his location, George would have been convinced he was dealing with an imbecile!

Fourth, even though the Narcissist will grant that such events also happen to other drivers, this does not lessen his sense of personal injury. "That doesn't matter," he seems to say. "Why is it happening to *me?*" In other words, the Narcissist is characterized by feelings of entitlement. Because of who he is, the good works he has done, the exemplary way he drives and so on, he should be spared such upsetting experiences.

Jay worked hard, saved diligently, and prided himself on the care he showed his mother and his generosity to children at Christmas. He believed he had earned the right to unobstructed travel. He took care of others; others should show the same consideration for him.

A fifth characteristic of the Narcissist is that he denies ever having committed the same act that, in others, enrages him. Jay never blocks passers, Peter never cuts in, Mike never impedes people in a hurry and George never hesitates. Of course they do, but they have no *awareness* of doing it. They are not conscious that their behavior can be so labeled. It would be abhorrent to them.

It is beyond the scope of this book to explain this paradox completely, but one key to it lies in the Narcissist's upbringing. The particular behavior that riles the Narcissist was not tolerated *in him* by parental figures when he was a child. Jay could not dally, Peter could not break the rules, Mike could not take it easy and George could not show signs of weakness.

The punishment for transgressing was severe. Consequently, when the Narcissist sees the prohibited behavior, it stirs up old pain and rage, which is vented on the perpetrator. Others might observe this same behavior in them, but the Narcissist cannot see it in himself (he cannot allow it in himself) or, if he sees it, he must excuse it or reclassify it under some other label.

Most of us have some of the Narcissist in us. Whenever we find ourselves thinking, "They shouldn't be allowed …!" we can add our name to the list.

The antidote for the Narcissist's feeling, "They shouldn't be allowed …" is "Live and let live." You must provide alternate points of view for the five characteristic attitudes and their underlying dynamics. What are these alternatives?

First, to lessen the pain caused by the memory of childhood trauma, *you must minimize the event.* Pay *less* attention to it. Don't take it in. Accept the fact that such things happen. The bumper sticker "Shit Happens" expresses this point of view exactly. Dwelling on the event tears you up.

Regard the stressor as just another happening in nature. Here's an illustration: suppose you were to set out for a hike across a wilderness area toward a distant mountain. On the way, you would anticipate certain obstacles. A swamp might block your route and force you to backtrack to find some way around it.

You wouldn't say, "They shouldn't allow swamps here!" You would accept swamps as part of nature and use your energy to solve the problem they present.

My suggestion is to take the same attitude toward highway travel. Just as there are swamps, boulders, streams, cliffs, brush and wild animals in nature, so are there obstacles on highways which are part of the world we live in. Any or all of the following are natural events on the highway:

- Fast-moving, packed three-lane interstates
- Traffic jams caused by traffic, construction or accidents
- Someone driving slowly
- Someone blocking a lane change
- Long lines at tollbooths
- Someone cutting into line
- Tailgaters
- Traffic lights not functioning properly
- Large trucks crowding your lane
- Someone angry at the way you drive

That's our highway world. Regarding such events in the same dispassionate way you regard nature will reduce your anger response. Shit happens!

When I first moved to Connecticut, weekend visits to New York City usually included being cheated out of some money — from five to twenty dollars. I felt badly about being duped until I accepted the fact that con men and petty cheats were more experienced than I. Once I mentally accepted this, and "budgeted" for being fleeced, I stopped overreacting. Similarly, accepting the inevitable delays, frustrations and even dangers of highway travel makes such occurrences less aggravating. It goes with the territory. If you're going to be part of the highway stream, it's better to go with the flow, expecting boulders, and "bumblers."

Next, accept the fact that you do not *know* the personality characteristics of the driver who offends you. The idea is nothing more than an illusion based on meager clues. Just as the Necker cube described earlier gives you insufficient data on how to decide which square is facing you, so the fleeting glimpse of the back of an offending driver's head, the person who suddenly cuts in front of you, provides insufficient data to decide her motivation.

You may have an instant conviction that she is an inconsiderate, reckless menace who shouldn't be allowed on the road, but she may be:

- A "he," who realized he was about to miss his turn.
- A woman trying to get her sick child to a doctor
- Someone swerving to avoid an accident
- An inexperienced driver who was unaware of your presence
- An experienced driver who didn't spot you because of a blind spot in her rearview mirror
- Someone who had been signaling properly from some distance, but had to force her way in because of discourteous drivers
- Someone fatigued from a long drive or stressful day
- Someone who simply believed she had a right to change lanes.

These scenarios (and more) are just as probable as yours, and you can curb your anger by assuming that *there is probably a good reason* for the behavior of the other drivers. In fact under similar circumstances, you might behave in the exact same way!

The fact is, most of the time the reason *is* understandable. Our *assumed* explanation most often is off the mark. Here are some examples:

A good friend of mine, David, who always hurries to get somewhere, told this story: "I was driving along 54th Street in Manhattan, when a young punk on the sidewalk shouted at me, 'Hey, Mister, your car is on fire!' I leaned out my window and yelled, 'Blow it out your a--!' A block later, I noticed smoke billowing out of my hood! It *was* on fire!"

A good example of prejudging an action!

One last, dramatic example appeared in the newspapers following the collapse of a section of the Mianus River Bridge in Greenwich, Connecticut. Two men speeding in a BMW saw a woman at the side of the road, apparently urging them to slow down as they started across the bridge. According to the woman, one of the men gave her the finger as they whizzed past. Moments later they hurtled to their deaths.

The moral: Assume that there is a good reason for other drivers' behavior. By so doing, you will diminish your stress reaction, and you might even save your own life!

IT'S NOT PERSONAL

Before going on the road, remind yourself that *highway encounters are not personal.* No one is exempt from unsettling incidents — they happen to everyone who drives. This reminder should help you offset your subjective feeling that traffic encounters are personal. They are not. The following suggestions may help:

Do not make eye contact with drivers who offend you, this will only escalate *your* urge to experience the event as personal. It won't be personal unless you make it so. My rearview mirror is adjusted so I cannot see the face of a tailgater. It's just another car on the road. This not only diminishes my anger, but the anger of the other driver as well. Human beings read signs of anger in other's faces, and will instinctively react defensively to the perceived threat. By avoiding the other driver's face, you disrupt the potential for escalating misunderstandings. Each of you is already reacting to faulty assumptions you have made about the other. The other driver does not know that you're eight months pregnant with your first child; you do not know that he has just been fired in a down-sizing. Don't look for trouble. Showing an angry, threatening or apprehensive face will only make matters worse.

Use your energies elsewhere. Most of these *perceived* personal affronts will disappear once you find something more interesting to do with your time. When you focus your attention on something to replace fault-finding, something just as compelling, the faults will fade and eventually disappear. You cannot focus on negative and positive values at the same time. Given a choice, the mind will eventually choose pleasure, assuming the "fault" does not pose any real danger.

Here are some better things to do with your driving time:
- Share interesting ideas with your companion
- Play highway games with your children
- Have someone read aloud excerpts from a book
- Listen to an endless variety of audio tapes
- Tune your radio to your favorite station

Doesn't it make more sense to focus on these?

Now that you have a better understanding of the Narcissistic style of driving, you're ready to make (your) three-by-five card containing old and new attitudes:

Old belief

Stressor: Another driver's faults
Urge: Lash out
            They shouldn't allow those
              a-- h---s on the road
            There's no excuse
            He's a menace, stupid and
              inconsiderate
            He's doing it on purpose
            He's wrong, I'm right

On the other side of the card write:

New Belief

Event: Another driver's faults
Urge: Understanding
            Live and let live
            Shit happens
            He probably has a good reason
            Just another obstacle to be solved
            I'll use my energy elsewhere

As with the other cards, review this each day before starting out, and after each time you react to events in the old way. Gradually, your old response will be extinguished.

Your old ways will die faster if you memorize your new beliefs, making them as readily accessible to you as the "Star Spangled Banner" is when the flag is raised at the beginning of some festivity.

Once you have joined your pet peeve to your new beliefs through memory, your rage at the image will fade. This will take about a month from the time you start. Storing your new reaction to the highway "event" by reviewing your three-by-five cards each time you react the old way will hasten the adoption of new attitudes.

The new attitudes grow over time. They grow because they make life more pleasurable. Given the choice between a bitter pill and a sweet one, human beings always choose the sweet one. But in order to do this you have to become aware of when to make the choice, and what the choice is about.

The Narcissist isn't aware that he has a choice. If you have Narcissistic tendencies, I hope I have been able to convince you that you *do* have a choice. I've shown you a method that will enable you to implement that choice.

I realize that personal resistance to developing new driving attitudes are bound to crop up. A common one is the thought, "I might overlook something dangerous to myself and others if I don't stay constantly on the lookout for the crazy a-- h---s I know are out there." Is there merit to this fear?

First of all, I am not suggesting you become oblivious to the real risks associated with driving. Following what I have proposed won't numb your brain. Indeed, I believe you will be able to spot real dangers more quickly when you are not so preoccupied with finding fault.

Driving an automobile is actually not very hard to do, indeed, it is quite easy. Most of the time, travel is safe and uneventful. The degree of agitation and threat that the Narcissist feels is far out of proportion to the real risks on the highway. I have devoted much of this chapter to explaining why this is so.

A driver *does* need to be attentive, and, above all, you must keep your eyes on the road. But preoccupation with fault-finding can itself be a distraction. Furthermore, it creates tension among your passengers, increasing that distraction.

Hypervigilance is not required to spot highway hazards, whether they are dangerous road conditions or dangerous drivers. Ordinary alertness will do.

Even so, accidents still happen.

One New Year's Eve, while I was still a resident in psychiatry at The Menninger Clinic, I was driving from Topeka to Kansas City to visit my wife, who was in the hospital. As I came over the top of a hill, I was suddenly confronted with another car's headlights coming right at me. I only had time to register this image before losing consciousness.

Sometime later I regained consciousness, dimly mindful of the sound of voices outside my car, and eventually, to the helping hands that brought me to the ambulance that took me to the hospital where my wife was a patient. Following surgery to repair my broken cheekbone and jaw, she and I shared "New Year's" when nurses brought her down to my room.

Was I the victim of someone who could be characterized as one of those "a-- h---s?" Yes, a drunk young man celebrating New Year's Eve drove the car I collided with. Could hypervigilance have prevented it? No. As a matter of fact, in those days *I was* on the lookout for "a-- h---s."

In the 36 years which have passed since my head-on collision, I have never witnessed an accident resulting in an injury. The chances are remote, so I continue to drive. I'm willing to take the chance. All of us who drive, walk, indeed *live,* take such chances.

The Narcissist, constantly on the lookout for "a-- h---s," is more at risk for such accidents than the normally alert drive.

However, the old beliefs and the concern they inspire will not go away entirely without the actual experience that the new beliefs work, and that nothing bad happens when you follow them. That's why I suggest you give yourself a month. It takes that much time on the road to really install the new beliefs in your mind, and to prove to yourself that following them does result in both a safer and more pleasurable journey.

Here's a "Burma Shave" jingle especially for the Narcissist:

Counting the wrongs
Of the way they drive
Causes blood pressure and gas
To boil inside.
Look for the right,
Let the wrongs be,
The rights will grow
Very pleasantly.

9

The Vigilante:
Teach 'em A Lesson

"Eye for eye, tooth for tooth,
Hand for hand, foot for foot."
Deuteronomy

I was a highway "Vigilante" once. Not the kind who chased offending drivers for a personal confrontation, but the kind who believed it was my duty to teach "bad" drivers a lesson by punishing them.

For slow drivers who blocked me from passing, I had a variety of vengeful strategies. When flashing my lights or honking my horn failed to motivate a driver, I fell back from the slow vehicle a bit and then accelerated as though I intended to ram him, stopping just short of his rear bumper. (I cannot remember actually doing this, but my son, tells me he can recall such occasions when he was about eight years old.)

At night I rode the slow driver's bumper with my high beams on.

I often passed the slow vehicles on the right, pulled in front of them, then abruptly slowed down, forcing them to brake sharply to avoid a collision.

A variation of this was to slow down to 30 miles per hour, or until I became the slow drivers' "slow driver." When they had had enough and had moved to their right to pass me, I would speed off, leaving them in my smoke, satisfied that I had "given them a taste of their own medicine."

I let tailgaters who rode my bumper with high beams blazing go by, then followed their cars closely with *my* high beams on.

Other tailgaters received my "quick-braking treatment." I depressed my brake pedal suddenly, forcing them to brake to avoid a collision, then at the last second I accelerated. This "punishment" served as a warning not to tailgate.

Lesser offenders received hand gestures, scornful looks, mouthed obscenities and blasts from my horn. Dr. Meyer Friedman, the pioneer in the treatment of heart attacks, aptly calls behavior like mine, "Being policeman to the world."

Besides having been a Vigilante myself, I have also been the victim of other Vigilantes. You may remember the incident I described earlier when a truck driver punished a friend and me on our way to play racquetball. He was a true Vigilante. More recently, I had an encounter with another Vigilante. I pulled up behind a car at a stoplight. It was a routine stop I'd made thousands of times on the way home from work over the last ten years. When the light changed I turned left following the same car. Suddenly, the car ahead of me abruptly stopped! I also halted, assuming a stray animal had darted across the road. After five seconds or so,

I realized there was no "stray animal" — the driver was punishing me; for what, I didn't know.

Annoyed, I reached for my pad to jot down the license number, but before I could, the car accelerated, spinning its wheels and roaring down the road. On reflection, I assume the driver thought my car came too close to his at the stoplight, although my stopping distance was the same as it has been since I began driving.

This past summer I vacationed in a small town in Idaho which had a right-of-way ordinance for pedestrians. One day I walked across the street, following a mechanic who I had asked to check my rented vehicle for a minor difficulty. In doing so I crossed well in front of an approaching line of cars coming along the street. The driver of the first vehicle honked his horn, rolled down his window, and shouted, "The next time you do that I'll run you over!"

Vigilante-style punishment is not always so benign. When the Vigilante meets the Vigilante, the result can be death. The *New York Times* recounted two such incidents this past year. In one, a Vigilante chased a Speeder, caught him, then forced him off the road. As he approached the Speeder's car to give him a piece of his mind, the Vigilante was confronted by several men in the car who shot him dead. In another incident, a man driving his wife to work chased a driver who had cut him off, pulled up beside him, and gave him the finger. The other driver took out a revolver and shot and killed the Vigilante's wife.

Vigilante-style punishment ranges from menacing words and gestures to murder. But all Vigilantes have one thing in common: they experience the "offense" of the other driver as *personally* offensive. Their intense response to traffic infractions makes them react as if they had been physically abused. They feel as if they have been struck and they want to hit back.

It's not hard to understand from where this reaction originates. It is the survival instinct in all animal species — fight or flight. You can read about it in Deuteronomy. You can hear it from parents when they instruct their children, who complain of being hit by other children, "Hit him back!" You can view it in thousands of movie and television programs where the plot repeatedly teaches that injury can only be resolved by inflicting greater injury on the perpetrators.

For the Vigilante to resign from his self-appointed role as "policeman to the world," he must come to realize that all these teachings are wrong, and not applicable to most highway experiences. Just as you cannot always believe your eyes (remember the Necker cube), you cannot always believe your "logical" conclusions. For example:

- Just because you feel like you have been personally injured, doesn't mean you have been.
- Just because you *conclude* the offending driver is a "bad" person, doesn't mean his is.
- Just because you *believe* it's in your best interest to hit back, doesn't mean it is.
- Just because you believe the other driver will *benefit* from the lesson you've taught her, doesn't mean she will.
- Just because you believe the incident has *spoiled* an otherwise pleasant journey, doesn't mean it has.

Most highway Vigilantes aren't Vigilantes in their interactions with other people off the highway. They know the five conclusions shown above aren't usually true. In fact, the thought might not even cross their minds. Why then do people who seem perfectly reasonable behave like dark avengers when they get behind the wheel? One answer is that they don't know enough about other drivers. Clues as to the personality of the other driver are minimal. Consequently, they are ruled by imagination, not facts. The way to change this is to replace imagined fears with knowledge and understanding.

When you witness "bad" driving, you must replace old beliefs, attitudes and assumptions with new ones. Let's examine those five beliefs that the Vigilante takes with him on the road.

Since it offends me, it must be personal. Most of the time, the highway Vigilante is the Narcissist who carries his feeling of personal injury to the next step — revenge.

True, to some degree you may be endangered by another driver's behavior. A tailgater poses real risks if you have to stop suddenly. A speeding car weaving from one lane to another at some distance poses only a remote threat to you, although such driving threatens the safety of others. In both cases, however, it's not personal; it's not directed at *you*.

Does this distinction make a difference? Yes, because if it *is* personal, you have much greater reason to be on your guard, or to prepare for fight or flight.

How do you decide whether it's personal? You can't decide solely on the basis of the pain endured; you must also evaluate the circumstances surrounding the painful experience.

For example, if you're walking in the woods and a hard object strikes your head, hurting you but neither drawing blood nor causing diminished consciousness, your first thought is likely to be, *"What* did that?" not *"Who* did that?" You think of acorns, not stones. You think of *impersonal* acts, not *personal* ones.

On the other hand, if you're walking on a battlefield in wartime, and a hard object strikes your helmet, your first thought, after running for cover, is apt to be *"Who* did that?" not *"What* did that?" You think of bullets, not acorns. You think of personal threats (someone is trying to kill me), not impersonal ones.

If you are a Vigilante, highway travel feels like a battlefield. In fact, it's much more benign. It's not as benign as a walk in the woods, but the only drivers who personally threaten you will be Vigilantes, and they will not actually threaten your life unless you take Vigilante-style action yourself.

Your stress level will be much lower if you remember that it's not personal when you see bad driving. You don't have to be a genius to drive a car. Expect to see all degrees of driving skill. Expect to see instances of bad judgement. That's just our highway world.

Bad drivers are "bad" people. This is another belief that Vigilantes hold dear. But most "bad" drivers look pretty much like you and me! In the movie, *The Wizard Of Oz,* there is a scene in the Emerald City in which Dorothy confronts the bumbling "wizard," hiding behind the curtain, and scolds him, "You're a *bad* man!"

The stammering wizard replies, "No, I'm a good man; just a very bad wizard!"

Most bad drivers are good men and women. They are just guilty of some bad driving.

Moreover, most "bad" drivers' *motives* are not reprehensible. In fact, practically all of them regard their motives as virtuous. A speeding driver most likely is trying to be on time for an appointment. A slow driver may be old and driving cautiously. Someone who cuts you off may believe she had to make an impulsive decision.

Yes, it is bad driving. Yes, it is poor judgement. But it is not malicious. The driver's "misdeed" was not the product of evil, destined to proliferate if not stopped.

Your stress level will be lower if you believe: "There's probably a good reason. I might drive that way myself in similar circumstances. It would be understandable if I knew the facts."

You won't lose your ability to recognize the minority of drivers who not only drive badly but *are* bad people. It's true that certain drivers, if given a chance, would rob, hurt and even kill. Others, high on drugs or alcohol, might crash into you. Stupid or otherwise, impaired drivers could wreck your car through negligence or bad judgement.

These are, indeed, a minority, and the wise response if you encounter them is not revenge, but to give them a wide berth — flight, not fight.

Don't let them get away with it — it's my duty to hit back. If you no longer regard the bad driving you witnessed as personally directed at you, or as the deed of a malicious person, what purpose does it serve for you to punish the driver?

By punishment, I mean intentional acts of retaliation beyond honking a horn. I refer to some act of retribution that penalizes, humiliates or injures the other driver.

These can range from several blasts of the horn, to shouting, swearing, gesturing and grimacing. Punishments include all those mentioned at the beginning of this chapter (attributed to yours truly) up to personal confrontation and physical injury. Even a curse uttered within the confines of your own car, which the other driver will never hear, is similarly motivated to make the offender "pay" for his offense.

While you can make the case for moral obligation to

go to the aid of a person being mugged, it's harder to justify punishing, for example, someone driving slowly or tail-gating. Unlike the mugger, the slow driver does not perceive her driving as "bad." She may believe she is within her rights, driving within the speed limit.

Indeed, she could easily think that the Vigilante's driving is "bad": a madman, endangering her comfort and safety! What the Vigilante intended as punishment could be perceived as an unprovoked attack. In this way, the Vigilante becomes the other drivers' "bad" driver.

By punishing, the Vigilante escalates his own anger and the anger of other drivers, thus raising the level of hostility that pollutes our nation's highways.

If you really wish to aid the police, jot down the offender's license number and send it with details to appropriate authorities. That would make sense, and it would show you're serious. Ask yourself whether your desire to punish is based on morality or on *revenge,* a desire to retaliate by venting your spleen on the "bad" person. The Vigilante as policeman, judge and executioner was outlawed long ago in civilized countries.

I gave up my "six-guns" long ago and retired from my role as policeman to the world. It's far better to leave punishment to the police. I now believe that it's not my business to punish.

Punishment will teach them a lesson — if you let them off it will get worse. Does Vigilante punishment improve driving skills by causing drivers to think twice about what they are doing? I doubt it. It doesn't make sense to believe an adult who is convinced he is in the right will let abuse from another driver convince him otherwise.

Advocates of punishment disagree. Not only do they point to parental use of punishment to curb unacceptable behavior in children, but to the legal system's use of police and jails as punishment to deter law breaking. Doesn't it stand to reason, they argue, that if we all punished "bad" drivers, highway manners would improve?

Again, I doubt it. Parents and police are culturally identified and culturally sanctioned authorities. Punishment, coming from someone other than a socially sanctioned "punisher" is not perceived as punishment at all, but as "sticking your nose in someone else's business."

Even as children, we defy punitive baby sitters with the shout, "You're not my mother!" And, as adults, if our peers reprimand us for something, our reply might be to suggest some place they could "stick it!" Authoritarian personalities without the badge or proper credentials have little effect in making discipline stick.

Remember, instead, that experience is the best teacher. By being the best driver you can be, you give the errant driver a model to learn from. Modeling is a far better teacher than punishment. Choose to teach by modeling. You'll be far more effective, and you'll make your journey more pleasant.

Bad drivers spoil my trip. This final belief of the Vigilante can happen only if you let it. If you overreact to every misdeed you see on the highway, blast the other driver and curse about the event over and over again to your passengers, *you* spoil your journey (and that of everyone else in your vehicle). If you downplay the event, treating it as just another problem to be solved, it will gradually fade in your awareness until it reaches proper proportions.

Since giving up the Vigilante business, my life on the road has been much more pleasant, peaceful and relaxed. My passengers are extremely grateful. We talk and laugh and play, now.

Further, I've noticed no deterioration in the driving expertise of other drivers since I retired. Indeed, quite the contrary, other drivers seem more courteous, and quite adept.

I wonder, "Could *I* have been the problem?"

As with other driving styles, you'll need help in practicing your new beliefs. To reinforce changing your attitude, write the following old and new belief on a three-by-five card:

Old Belief

Stressor: A "bad" driver
Urge: Punish
             Teach him a lesson
             Give him a taste of his own
                 medicine
             Don't let him get by with it
             He's a bad person
             He'll spoil my trip

On the other side, write:

New Belief

Stressor: Driver endangering me or others
Urge: Problem-solve
             Leave punishment to the police
             My punishing only aggravates
             Model good driving
             He probably has good reason
             Give him a wide berth

Practice countering all five old assumptions. For example, imagine you are driving in the middle lane of a highway, when someone abruptly cuts in front of you from the left, forcing you to apply your brakes. Then he speeds on, making another lane change to gain more ground, cutting in front of another vehicle up ahead. You say:

"No need to punish, leave that to the police, he's probably a good person, rushing to be on time, trying to keep his commitments. Let's give him a wide berth."

It's not always easy to do. Memorization of your new beliefs is important along with practice. The combination will dissipate most of your rage and allow you to turn your attention away from the person who cut you off, and back to enjoying the road.

Here's my "Burma Shave" jingle for Vigilantes:

Gil gave a finger to Jill,

Jill said f--- y-- to Phil,

Phil said a-- h--- to Mil,

Mil said s-- of a b---- to Will,

And so goes the dance of ill-will.

10

Putting It All Together

"No psychic value can disappear without being replaced by another of equal intensity."
Jung

Imagine driving with these five passengers:
  Speeder
  Competitor
  Passive-Aggressor
  Narcissist
  Vigilante

Speeder urges you to make good time by traveling as fast as you can go.

Competitor cheers you on to be number one, by engaging in made up contests with other drivers.

Passive/Aggressor insists you block any drivers who threaten to win these contests, even if it means denying them their right of way.

Narcissist keeps up an angry diatribe about the faults

of other drivers, continually shouting and pointing out all the a-- h---s that shouldn't be allowed on the road.

Vigilante coaches you in ways to teach bad drivers a lesson by punishing them for the way they drive.

Do you want them as passengers? Can you imagine the continual uproar inside your vehicle? Think of the hostility level! Consider the stress you would feel. Who would you ask to leave first?

You might ask Vigilante to leave first; he is apt to cause the most serious trouble by "punishing" another armed Vigilante. Then, in order to make things quieter and less hostile you drop Narcissist off. After that Passive/Aggressor is removed, probably kicking and screaming, because she is always causing trouble with other drivers who want their right of way. That leaves Competitor and Speeder, and of the two, Competitor is the most troublesome by creating conflicts (he would call them contests), where none need to exist. Out he goes.

That leaves Speeder, who seems harmless enough until you decide to slow down, after narrowly missing a cow standing in the road as you come around a bend. At this point, Speeder begins to nag you to drive faster, so you leave her at the side of the road.

Of course, changing your driving habits is not that easy. First, since the "passengers" are all linked inside your head, they cannot be dealt with one at a time. For example, you cannot let go of Speeder without also letting go of Competitor. Second, you can't let go of any of these completely — just like that. You may be able to stop competing at the beginning of a long journey, when you are fresh and encounter'little traffic, but later in the day, when you are tired and driving through a city with bumper-to-bumper traffic, you may resume being competitive.

The third difficulty in this process is that your "passengers" don't simply leave; they have to be replaced by more congenial companions. That is the lesson from Jung who said the brain cannot stop doing something unless it is replaced with something else. Finally, letting go of these "passengers" follows a different sequence when you are trying to change your behavior. Vigilante cannot leave first. Vigilante is only the ultimate consequence of a chain reaction that begins with Speeder. It's easiest to start with Speeder, closely followed by Competitor.

When I started this process myself, I initially decided to drive slower to please a nervous passenger. But, I could only do it for a short time before I became irritable. For a while I couldn't understand why this should be, until I realized I was reacting to all the "contests" I was losing to the cars passing me. Each vehicle that whizzed by took me further away from the competitive edge to be Number One.

All of the stressful highway attitudes are similarly connected. Consequently, you must set off prepared to change all five attitudes if you're going to be successful in curbing your highway hostility. One way to do this is to carry all five three-by-five cards with you. Review them each morning, and again each time you overreact. Gradually, the new beliefs will click into your mind.

As I said, your undesirable passengers will not leave all at once. They depart one at a time and in degrees. Allowing yourself more time driving to work partially eliminates the Speeder, although you may still rush on the three-hour weekend drive to a ski lodge. Next, you decide not to tailgate slow drivers in the left lane, but simply pass them on the right. Once past, you refrain from punishing them by slowing down in front of them. Exit one Narcissist and one Vigilante. Then, when there's a traffic jam, you decide to stop jumping from lane to lane to get ahead of other cars. Out goes one Competitor and another aspect of the Speeder. At a point where two lanes merge you allow a car from the other lane to nudge in front of you. Goodbye Passive-Aggressor. And so it goes. The undesirables leave one at a time, slowly at first. But as you become more aware of them you will carry fewer of them with you, and they will gradually lose their influence.

The "disappearance of the undesirables" requires further revision to be completely accurate. The old ways don't fall into disuse and lose their power immediately, not finally, until they are replaced by equally compelling values. Hence, Speeder leaves when Good Time enters. Good Time loves to laugh, tell jokes, and discuss interesting topics. He is more interested in enjoying the journey than rushing to the destination.

Competitor leaves as Being Number One retires in favor of Cooperation; and Passive/Aggressor is replaced by Courtesy: Narcissist exits as Compassion enters; Vigilante has much less to do when Narcissist departs and soon makes way for Common Sense, who leaves punishment to the police.

Although you must deal with each of these behaviors as they come up, you will find that they diminish as you reduce the importance of making good time (Speeder) and being number one (Competitor). The reason for this is that we are programmed during childhood to think in terms of do's, don'ts and consequences. Speeder and Competitor represent the do's; the values you are driving by *(living by* on the road). Passive/Aggressor and Narcissist represent the don'ts; what you (and others) are prohibited from doing. (Don't lose. Don't drive like that.)

The Vigilante represents the consequences for failing

to live up to the do's and for participating in the don'ts. The programmed consequence is some form of punishment. As you reduce the importance of making good time and being number one, there are fewer don'ts to avoid. If you are no longer speeding, there is less reason to fault yourself for not making good time. You are also less angry at the traffic tie-ups. The highway maintenance workers, who have closed one lane, causing a problem, cease being a-- h---s. Also, if you've stopped making up competitive contests, you'll allow others to pass you without being resentful of them or mad at yourself.

As Passive/Aggressor and the Narcissist quiet down, Vigilante has fewer occasions to punish. Just as emphasis on making good time and being number one set in motion an escalating cycle of increasing stress, so their de-emphasis sets in motion an escalating cycle of increasing harmony, peacefulness and good cheer.

You will find it easier to put it all together if you learn a relaxation response technique. Because methodologies for acquiring this skill are widely available, I will not elaborate on any particular approach. I recommend the works of Jon Kabot-Zinn and Herbert Benson. Shifting from the old beliefs to the new beliefs can be greatly facilitated by prac-ticing while in an altered state of consciousness brought about through a simple relaxation, breathing and focusing exercise.

It's similar to shifting the gears of a car. In order to go from one gear to the next, the transmission must be placed in neutral by engaging the clutch. Only then can you move easily to another gear.

The relaxation response fulfills the same function as the clutch when it comes to shifting values. You must stop being driven by one before you can begin moving to another. Most of the time, we race from our work to our cars, in which we race to our homes, where we race through our chores, running by with hardly a glance at our relationships. We only disengage on a vacation, and there it takes three to eight days to slow down and adopt another way of going through the day. The relaxation response is a skill that allows you to disengage anytime you have five to fifteen minutes to devote to it. Even though the time is short, the contemplation of new beliefs during this period (and, better yet, memorizing them while in this state of mind) increases the rate at which the old undesirable passengers get out of the car and the new companions get in.

Try it! Reserve fifteen minutes for yourself. Pick a quiet spot, where you won't be disturbed. Take your five cards, and proceed as follows. Suppose you want to reduce your overreaction to tailgaters:

- Elicit the relaxation response.
- Visualize or imagine a tailgater.
- Read your list of new beliefs.
- Elicit the relaxation response.
- Visualize or imagine the tailgater.
- Read your list of of new beliefs.
- Try to remember them.
- Elicit the relaxation response.

Doing this with each highway stressor you overreact to will gradually extinguish your hostility. It's that simple.

Gradually, pleasurable highway attitudes will begin to take hold. These, too, will become intertwined and mutually reinforcing. You'll drive to "make time good" and treat yourself and passengers like "Number One beings!" Delays afford you opportunities to further relax your vigilance and concentrate on pleasurable experience. You'll find yourself courteous and considerate of other vehicles needing to pass.

Learning new driving attitudes is no different than acquiring any new skill. Study, memorize and practice until you incorporate the knowledge. With time, the new attitudes will feel familiar and will be a source of self-esteem.

Your automobile will become a port in the storm.

11

When The Other Driver Is Hostile

"Anger blows out the lamp of the mind."
Ingersoll

A 1987 study of 137 Los Angeles highway firearm assaults identified as most common the following trigger events: tailgating, impeding traffic and merging or lane changing

Long after your own usual level of highway anger has diminished, you can still be enraged anew by another driver's fury at you. It's understandable that rage in another person triggers an alarm reaction in you — the person wants to harm you in some way. Remember the anger intensity scale I displayed early in the book? It showed how a person's anger can be ranked from zero (contentment) to ten (killing rage). The scale told us that if another driver's anger is noticeable from his automobile, it's at least at a seven. Chances are you're dealing with a Vigilante who believes you deserve punishment and is driving his car in some way to do just that. Since you don't know to what lengths he is prepared to go, you automatically become aroused, vigilant, and get ready for fight or flight. True, he may be getting ready only to mouth an obscenity or give you the finger, but you don't know; he might have a gun.

In this chapter I will suggest attitudes and strategies for you to use when you are confronted by drivers engaged in any of the three triggering events listed above. But first, some general principles:

- Accept the fact that you're bound to meet a Vigilante someday. That way you will be less affronted when it happens.
- Don't take it personally. Although it feels personal, it's not *you* the angry driver is mad at. It could be anybody he thinks is obstructing what he wants to do.
- Play it down. Stay cool. Don't make it a big deal.
- Remember, in most cases the angry driver is not truly dangerous and will not physically harm you, especially if you don't escalate and retaliate.
- There's probably a good reason he is driving the way he is.
- Recall Ingersoll's words: "Anger blows out the lamp of the mind." He's not playing with a full deck.
- View him as desperate and anxious not as a challenger. Give him a wide berth. The highway is no place for petty squabbles.
- Avoid eye contact; that keeps it impersonal.
- If he escalates, get out of there. He may be dangerous. Go for help; find a policeman.
  Now, on to the specifics.

TAILGATING

Tailgating is dangerous! One morning, on my commute into New York during rush hour, I saw in my rearview mirror that a car was rapidly approaching. The driver flashed her lights several times and tailgated me, obviously in a desperate hurry. I had an opportunity to pull over into the middle lane and did just that. As she sped by, hard on her heels was another tailgater and after that car, yet another, and after that a fourth and a fifth. They moved as a unit, each one pushing the one in front, scarcely two feet apart. Zip – zip – zip – zip – zip.

A few minutes later, as I approached the neighborhood of Yankee Stadium, the traffic became congested and slowed to a crawl. The far left lane was completely stopped, and all of us had to squeeze into the two right lanes. Soon the cause for the obstruction came into view: the five tailgaters had run into each other when the lead vehicle braked suddenly to avoid hitting a car that swerved in front of her. Crash – crash – crash – crash!

The presence of real imminent danger distinguishes tailgating from other highway stressors. Multivehicle accidents are common. Unaware of the danger, the tailgater is singularly focused on speeding to his or her destination. Often, the tailgater is a victim of an illusion created by a feeling of "safety in numbers." "Everybody" seems to be speeding, it's the thing to do. Come on gang, let's pass those dawdlers!

In addition to finding tailgaters on high-speed expressways, there are two other circumstances where you are apt to encounter them: two-lane roads and when slowing down on any street to make a turn. In the first two circumstances the tailgaters are Speeders, while in the last instance, even slow drivers may inadvertently become tail-gaters when you slow down to make a turn.

The sense of alarm you feel with a tailgater comes from more than just the real danger. You also can sense the tailgater's mood. A perceptive driver can tell the difference between a car that simply wants to pass and the hostile tailgater. How a driver flashes his lights, blows his horn or approaches you conveys his emotional state. Some "ask" to pass, some "expect" to pass, some "insist" on passing, and some desperately *"demand"* to pass *"or else!"*

It's helpful in managing your emotions to think of the tailgater as a person who is being transformed from a kindly Dr. Jekyll, speeding along to his destination, to a dangerous Mr. Hyde. The process takes four steps:

1. The self-esteem of a well-intentioned Dr. Jekyll (alias Speeder) is dependent on achieving certain driving goals, usually to reach a destination by a set time or to maintain a certain speed.

2. Failure to achieve these goals (your vehicle is an obstacle) transforms Dr. Jekyll into the Competitor who feels his self-esteem is threatened when he thinks he is *losing,* producing a painfully depressed mood.

3. The Narcissist emerges in Dr. Jekyll's continuing alteration. Since you and your car are deemed responsible for the *bad* driving that hinders him from meeting his goals, you are regarded as an a- - h---, beneath contempt.

4. Mr. Hyde (alias Vigilante) takes over and seeks a method to punish you, to make your life miserable. The longer he has to wait, the more his rage mixes with a mounting sense of desperation.

It's this combination of desperation and anger in tail-gaters, together with your own awareness of real risk that can cause you to feel both anger and fear. Should you fight or flee? When you can't decide you feel overwhelmed and slightly confused. What to do?

1. Don't look at the tailgater or his car. Ordinarily you would look behind and keep an eye on danger, but in this case you're safer not to. Usually, tailgaters are competent drivers, so you don't have to watch them like a hawk. By avoiding eye contact, you'll make it less personal for both of you and without that element of personal challenge you'll be calmer and more in control of your car.

    I adjust my rearview mirror so I can see at a glance the right half of the car behind me but I cannot see the driver's face (nor can he see mine).

2. Don't speed up, or slow down. Drive like a state trooper: real steady. If the way you drive your car is not affected by his presence, he is more apt to calm down, or, realizing that he cannot influence you, he'll pass you on the right. If he senses any fear or panic on your part he will press you harder. If he senses that you're going to fight him, he'll rise to the challenge.

3. Concentrate on driving your car and, when safe, pull over and let him pass. He wants to go faster than you do, so let him. This may be hard for you to do graciously if you resent his rudeness. You may be tempted to punish him by denying him the right-of-way. It will be easier if you take one of the following points of view:
    *   More than likely there is a "good reason" he

wants to pass. He may be trying to keep an
urgent appointment.

- He represents a danger to you; give him a
  wide berth.
- Don't let his rudeness erode your courtesy.
  Say, "Be my guest!" and give him the road.
- Even "bad guys" have a right to pass. Move
  over!

You also may have difficulty yielding the right-of-way
if you perceive his challenging manner as a personal threat
to your self-esteem. But it's important to see him as
desperate rather than *menacing*. He is more like a cornered
animal than a schoolyard bully. While cornered animals can
inflict serious damage, your attitude and response should be
different than it would be to a schoolyard bully. Bullies
respect you more if you stand up to them; cornered animals,
treated aggressively, just become more desperate.

Under these circumstances, a firm, cautious, no-
nonsense attitude is more effective. You carefully make it
possible for the animal to go free without hurting him or
yourself. Or, to use another metaphor, you keep your gun on
the drunken cowboy who wants to fight you as you back out
of the saloon. Remember:

This is a trivial matter.

It's not worth dying for.

Use your energies elsewhere.

Choose better battles, not this one.

But, what about those situations where you can't pull
over, or where it's not in your interest to do so? There are
three of these: making a turn, driving on a busy two-lane
road with no place to pull over and driving on any road

where you are also trying to make the best possible time.

First, you're slowing to make a turn, but the car behind you keeps coming on. You instinctively hesitate to apply brakes too strongly for fear he won't be able to stop, thereby causing a collision. However, by not slowing down you risk making your turn much too fast, resulting in too wide a turn, which may cause you to collide with another car.

Anyone who drives so closely behind another vehicle that he cannot stop or swerve in an emergency loses some measure of his or her sensitivity, compassion and good judgement. A sensitive, aware person will slow down and back off when his vehicle comes too close to another. However, if a diligent driver is surprised by a vehicle that suddenly slows down in front of him, bringing the two vehicles too close, fear may cause a normally courteous driver to lash out.

If you want to make a turn, and there are vehicles close behind you, it is essential that you give them plenty of warning and convey to them that you are a flesh-and-blood human being with aspirations of your own; not just an inanimate "obstacle." Your messages must say:

- I'm for real.
- I'm going to make a turn.
- I'm troubled by your closeness.
- I wish you'd back off.
- I'm determined to make a safe turn.

Here's how to send these messages:

1. Put your turn indicator on very far in advance of where you intend to turn. That gives plenty of time for the message to register.

2. Slow down far in advance of where you want to make the turn. You want to overcome potential insensitivity, so start early and avoid surprises.

3. Adjust your rearview mirror if the driver behind you continues to be too close. This will be enough to cause fifty percent of inadvertent tailgaters to slow down. The Speeder will read your mood from the way you adjust your mirror.

4. Avoid eye contact; don't speed up. Make yourself concentrate on your driving.

5. Continue to depress your brake pedal just enough to light up your tail lights, so you can control your slowing without coming to a crawl as you approach your corner.

6. If the driver continues to be close, roll down your window and use an arm signal (not a finger signal).

7. Concentrate on making the best turn you've ever made in your life. Vigilantes may roar around you at the last minute, and some may toot their horns, but that's their problem, not yours. Most drivers will be courteous if you follow these steps.

A second situation where it's difficult to allow a tailgater to pass is on a busy two-lane road. Here, either oncoming traffic or the absence of a sufficient straightaway precludes an impatient tailgater from passing. Nonetheless, he persists in driving too closely.

Usually, the steps I've described up to now will be sufficient to curb your anxiety or anger. Both you and the tailgater are seemingly trapped by circumstance. If *you* can live with it, and send him the messages mentioned above, he may calm down and resign himself to being late.

However, if she persists and continues to press, assume there's probably a good reason. Pull over to the side of the road and wave her by. Your own journey will be much more pleasant. It's no big deal.

Believe it or not, there is a place where tailgaters have the right-of-way! On St. John Island in the Caribbean, the roads have two lanes, very winding and hilly, with virtually no straightaways. As a consequence, the law states that if someone wants to pass, you must pull off the road and let him.

Under these circumstances, tailgaters are more patient; they know you will pull over when it's safe, so they are less desperate and pushy. Likewise, for the person who pulls over there is no loss of face; he's simply being law abiding.

You can adopt the same attitude even though you're not in the Virgin Islands. However, there is a third situation, which can further complicate your decision. You're either in the left lane of a crowded six-lane interstate, or on a two-lane road. Traffic congestion slows all cars, and you'd like to go faster. You're late and don't want further delays. A tailgater flashes his high beams behind you, then leaves them on high.

The mounting danger you feel in this situation conflicts with your desire to remain in it in order to reach your destination on time. Once again, do you fight or flee? Remember, you have a third choice:

Communicate, and stay the course.

Follow all the steps just described, remaining steady on course (like a state trooper), without panicking or retaliating. If you can remain cool, accepting this as just one of those unavoidable situations from living in a crowded metropolitan community, the tailgater may become resigned, too. If you're not willing to play the role of either "victim" or "combatant," the tailgater will have to look for someone else with whom to play his dangerous game.

IMPEDING TRAFFIC

Hostility can be encountered in the Passive/Aggressor almost as much as in the Speeder. One of the sweetest little old ladies you can imagine complained to me about the vicious tailgaters who made her life miserable on a daily basis. Initially, I was sympathetic, but when I became puzzled by the number of tailgaters she found on the highway, I asked her to describe her experience in more detail. It turned out that she drove 30 MPH! A character right out of *Arsenic and Old Lace,* she couldn't understand why drivers were perturbed by her *safe* driving.

You often encounter slow drivers who refuse to yield the right-of-way and let you pass, even though there are no vehicles stopping them from pulling over. Understanding who they are helps you to devise an approach that keeps your own frustration at a minimum.

Speeder: Naturally, if the driver who is a problem for you is a Speeder, it means that you are one, too. If you come up behind him, wait patiently until he can pull over into an open lane. Usually, he's driving very fast anyway and will go even faster with you urging him on. He doesn't want to decrease *his* rate of travel, however, and will not yield the right-of-way until he can do so without slowing down. Then, after he allows you to pass, he'll return to the passing lane behind *your* car, increase his speed, and you both will go whizzing along.

Competitor: In the case of the driver who is a Competitor, (which of course you won't know until he shows his colors) approach from behind slowly but steadily, so he doesn't feel you have a personal investment in besting him. Be patient. If he doesn't feel you're in a contest, courtesy may prevail and he'll yield. Failing this, flashing your lights may get him to go faster. He may decide to compete with you by staying ahead. In order to "beat" you, he may increase his speed, thereby accomplishing your objective of traveling faster, without *having* to pass.

Passive/Aggressor: If you approach slowly, in all cases, you'll confront fewer frustrating situations. In the case of the Passive-Aggressor, be patient and respectful as you pull up behind him. After a while, you'll become familiar to him and if you seem like a "nice guy," he'll let you go by. Flashing your lights, honking your horn, or tail-gating may cause him to become more intransigent, or even to slow down in order to frustrate you more. Rather than continuing to press and getting into a protracted struggle, simply pass on the right. When you do pass, do it decisively and quickly so that there's no chance for a contest. If you pass too gradually, he may gradually escalate, as well.

Narcissist: The arrogance and feelings of entitlement of the Narcissist render him unable to accommodate the needs of others. It's best to simply pass on the right. It's not worth the struggle.

Vigilante: The particular type of Vigilante who refuses to yield the right-of-way is one I call the Policeman. If the posted speed is 55, then, by God, he is going to go 55 in the left lane, and he's going to make sure that *no one* breaks the law! Signal once with your lights that you want to pass, but be patient and don't press. Even drop back a bit. Act law abiding! Going up a hill, he may slow down and pull over. However, if there is no reason for him to slow down, you're in for a long speed-limit ride. Once it's clear to you that you're dealing with a Policeman, either relax and tag along, or pass on the right. He ain't going to budge!

MERGING OR LANE CHANGING

You are apt to encounter hostile drivers in the following situations:
- At tollbooth lines, either cutting in, or trying to keep you from cutting in.
- Entering an expressway.
- Changing lanes on an expressway.
- When two lanes merge into one.

"Chicken" is the most common game played on highways, and, in most circumstances, is played when one vehicle tries to enter a moving line of traffic. So long as skilled drivers play fair, take turns and exercise courtesy, there is little problem. But the hostile driver who does not want to take turns or play fair creates a real danger. How should you contend with the driver trying to cut in ahead of his turn, or the driver who won't let you in?

Remember that accidents can happen in split seconds in these circumstances, so be especially alert and prepared when you enter an expressway, change lanes or merge with another lane. These are high risk situations. *Don't treat them casually.* They require your most skillful driving! We do them so often they become old hat, but you can never predict when the unexpected will happen. Stay alert.

Confrontations may occur, but because of the extreme danger for a fender bender, adopt the following attitudes:
- Give the other person the benefit of the doubt.
- It's not worth dying for.
- Be patient, you'll get there soon enough.

- It's not a referendum on your self-worth.
- Treat it as a trivial matter
- Don't compete. Wait for a more courteous driver.

When you combine your ability to react less angrily to hostile drivers with your ability to put it all together, you'll notice your pleasure in driving increases enormously.

The Los Angeles study didn't cover one additional circumstance in which you may encounter a hostile driver: right in the front seat next to you, your spouse! What if he or she is the hostile driver? What can you do if your spouse rants and raves about the way other drivers drive, or the stupid design of the highways?

By now you know that certain approaches don't get very far. Asking him to slow down may increase his anger and some of it may get redirected at you, together with justifications for the need to make good time. Asking him to stop ranting and raving similarly causes him to shift some of his anger toward you, complete with self-righteous indignation. After all, *he's* not the one driving like a dangerous imbecile, *they* are!

Simple requests meet only limited success because he cannot *stop* doing anything; he can only *start* doing some alternative. Therefore, to get your mate to change requires suggesting alternatives for him to start.

Another reason these approaches fail is bad timing. Before he can even *comprehend* an alternative, he must be in a mood to consider alternatives. Talking to him while he battles other drivers won't get his full attention. The focus of his anger prevents him from seeing other options. You must lay the groundwork when he can better contemplate options. You wouldn't wait for a fire before telling someone what to do in case of one.

The hostile driver's attitude, like a fireman fighting a fire, focuses on dealing with something he perceives as a threat. Suggesting that he experiment with new approaches at that point will place him in danger (from his point of view) of losing the battle. He, rightly, won't want to risk it.

The best time to talk to a spouse about this problem (and it is *his* problem) is during a time of peace and harmony between you. Though the subject may irritate him, he will have better ability to control his irritation since no current threat exists (the other drivers).

The second best time to talk to your spouse is the day before going on a drive. This gives him time to weigh the alternative you've presented. The third best time occurs just after a journey when he has calmed down, but still has the fresh memory of his most recent highway encounters.

Before talking to him, make sure you thoroughly understand the concepts put forward in this book. Framing his problem in the way described will greatly enhance your effectiveness. Having *conviction* about the nature of his problem and *conviction* about how to solve it makes you sound more confident and believable. The more you believe in what you're suggesting, the more convincing you will sound and be. Whining, merely complaining or nagging won't work.

Another word about timing. Many people are reluctant to choose a harmonious time because you *know* the hostile driver will get mad. But after you face the tempest he will probably be in a better mood to *hear* about driving alternatives.

There is no way out of it. He will not change without a struggle. If you choose not to struggle, you choose a life of enduring hostility. Your choice is to pick the time when the odds are on your side, when he is least defensive and most open to consider your wishes and desires. If you plan your campaign well, couched in terms of what you want, and you persist, the hostile driver will change.

While a time of harmony may be best for your confrontation, the period just before a journey may be easiest. This could be before a routine short trip, such as grocery shopping, dining out, going to the movies or visiting friends or relatives. The idea is that you may be able to convince him to change his ways for a short journey. This is not as threatening to him as a total attitude change.

The strategy to use on the hostile drivers of the world can be described in five topics. Here they are, along with typical arguments you might use to convert him to more pleasurable driving:

TOPIC ONE: CHANGING THE HOSTILE DRIVER'S ATTITUDE FROM MAKING GOOD TIME TO MAKING TIME GOOD

"Honey, when we make our next journey let's plan a more leisurely trip. Instead of trying to get there in twenty minutes, let's allow thirty. That way we can talk together and enjoy each other. I get frightened and annoyed when we rush. I don't like it. You get irritable, you're not as much fun as you used to be. Let's try to get the old days back. I bought a new cassette I know you'll enjoy. Besides, there's something I'd like to talk to you about."

You get the idea. Whatever his response, keep promoting your campaign to make time together good. If he argues for the necessity of speed, don't directly challenge his assertion. Simply point out that it is incompatible with listening to the tape together, conversing, watching scenery, or engaging in other activities. They can't be relished while

rushing. Say to him: "We don't have to rush. I hate rushing."
Emphasize, over and over, what the advantages are.

TOPIC TWO: CHANGING THE HOSTILE DRIVER'S ATTITUDE FROM BEING NUMBER ONE TO TREATING BOTH OF YOU AS NUMBER ONE BEINGS

Since automobile commercials emphasize speed and
invite drivers to compete, you will have to exert at least
equal effort to promote comfort, fun and treats. Buy attrac-
tive travel cups, picnic baskets, cassette holders, personal
decorations on the dashboard, memorabilia on the windows,
vases to hold flowers and irresistible treats. When our
children were small, I referred to treats as "emergency
rations." Emergencies were frequently declared!

Here are some more ideas for suggesting to your
partner a new way of doing things:

"For your trip tomorrow, let's get the car washed and
cleaned inside. I'm going to make some sandwiches, and I
bought some gum and other treats."

"Let's stop at the drive-in on the way for some coffee.
I enjoy making our trips fun."

"Do me a favor. Don't be so concerned with racing
other cars. That takes away from my comfort and interest."

"I bought a new tape for you — it's one of your
favorites."

Good times don't just happen, you've got to make
them happen. First-class treatment isn't automatic; you've
got to know what it looks like, communicate your vision,
and campaign to make it a reality.

These first two topics are the most important ones.
When you're successful with these, the next three topics
won't come up. However, to bring about the change, all

topics may have to be discussed.

TOPIC THREE: CHANGING THE HOSTILE DRIVER'S ATTITUDE TOWARD OTHER DRIVERS WHO SEEK THE RIGHT-OF-WAY

Review the chapter on the Passive-Aggressor. Reacquaint yourself with the point of view he will most likely advance for his defense. Remember the example of Roy, who felt that he would be a "loser" if he yielded the right-of-way. Being mindful of that, emphasize how much more you admire him for being courteous, which helps to promote your partner's self-esteem. By minimizing his negative qualities while maximizing your respect for his virtues, you make it easier for him to change his point of view. Talk about what he does right, not what he does wrong. Being critical of him only increases the bad feelings he already has about himself. Say, "I really admire your courtesy," not "why don't you learn how to drive?"

TOPIC FOUR: CHANGING THE HOSTILE DRIVER'S BELLIGERENCE TOWARD OTHER DRIVERS' MISCUES

Changing the Narcissist takes a greater effort than changing the Speeder. The Narcissist sees faults in others; the Speeder reacts only when his targeted goal threatens to elude him. Knowing that the Narcissist fights awareness of his own faults, suggesting that he be more tolerant of others also helps him to become more tolerant of himself. Suggesting ways in which your time together can be more enjoyable for *you* invites him to move away from his pain toward activities that make *him* feel good. Arguing about the merits of each fault he sees will get nowhere. Labeling him a "fault finder" and asking him to stop it or keep it to himself works better providing you consistently do so *each* time it happens, and really mean it. This means that if he persists beyond a certain point, you must refuse to ride with him.

The most frequent reason people give for resisting doing this is, "I'd be doing it all the time." That's not true. Consistent opposition does work. Consider a child who persists in running across the street without looking. If a parent reprimands him only every fourth time she witnesses it the behavior is unlikely to change because she tacitly condones the other three times. To motivate the child to change, the aversive conditioning must occur every time the behavior is observed. In addition, the parent needs to go to the street with the child, model the correct behavior and demonstrate the danger by experiencing a car racing by. It takes that much for the risk to sink in. While your partner is not a child, he may not change until he knows that the alternative is the loss of your companionship.

TOPIC FIVE: CHANGING YOUR SPOUSE'S ATTITUDE FROM TEACH 'EM A LESSON, TO LEAVE PUNISHMENT TO THE POLICE

Punishing other drivers risks both of your lives. And today, there is a real risk that the other driver may have a gun. You must put your foot down on this one (if you haven't done so before). The ultimate choice you can give your spouse — stop punishing people and have your companionship, or continue his dangerous behavior without you — must be seriously considered. I have treated several hostile men who curbed their sanguine attitudes when their wives really meant it, and actually refused to accompany their husbands until they changed. One such fellow used to watch two football games simultaneously on two television sets. Afterward, he was in such a rage because of his disappointment with his football teams that his wife refused to ride with him.

He transferred his rage into unsuitable behavior behind the wheel. He told me that because of his wife's refusal to ride with him he learned a relaxation technique, which he employed for 20 minutes after the football games. It calmed him down enough so that he could be civil with other drivers. It was only then that his wife rejoined him in the car.

Rome wasn't built in a day. A new language cannot be learned in one sitting. But Rome *was* built and new languages *are* learned. Your spouse can learn new ways, too. With persistence and determination, you can show him the way.

12

Driver Safety Report Cards

"Union gives strength."

Aesop

Does the Vigilante have a point? Is there a need for some form of direct community participation to insure responsible driving?

Much as we abhor the Vigilante who takes matters into his own hands and acts as police, jury, judge and executioner, there is a kernel of sense in his behavior. Through the ages, community censure has been an extremely effective way to foster citizen compliance with community standards and values. One of the most powerful behavioral influences among the various diverse ethnic groups that formed our country were centuries-old traditions that conveyed, *"We* don't do things *that* way; we do things *this* way."

Up to this point, we have no such tradition to guide our behavior on the highway. We need to establish that tradition. We need to get together and decide to establish responsible driving behavior on our highways. It is possible to accomplish this. In Switzerland, if a pedestrian crosses a street before the traffic light signals "Walk," other pedestrians will converge on him, urging compliance with the law.

It's easy to see why we have not formed a tradition of driving responsibly. Automobile driving has been with us only a short time compared to, say dining together. We know what's expected when we eat together; there are thousands of years of traditions. Not so with driving. And, as a culture has evolved, the responsibility for enforcing community values has shifted from collective community action to delegated representatives of the community, like the police.

The result of this shift has fostered an unhealthy split; the average citizen-driver feels (and is) less involved and responsible for enforcing community values. Indeed, quite the contrary, there exists a strong anti-police attitude among drivers, voiced by such sentiments as; "Mind your own business," "It's not my problem," and "Don't be a squealer." While a Vigilante may personally try to punish another driver, he is not apt to report that driver to the police so that designated community authorities can evaluate the incident and mete out appropriate punishment.

This anti-police sentiment echoes the taunt from my childhood, "tattle-tale, tattle-tale." Don't tell the grown-ups. Strange as it may seem, most drivers are loath to report even dangerous drivers to police.

Of course, in defense of Vigilantes and passive bystanders, right now there is no convenient methodology for filing a report with the police. There is no avenue for enabling such a tradition to flourish.

I believe there is a relatively simple, easy and low cost

method for establishing this tradition. I refer to Driver Safety Report Cards. Here's how they work.

Under this plan, each licensed driver would receive five Driver Safety Report Cards per year from the Motor Vehicle Department of the state issuing the license. On one side would be the address of the motor vehicle department. The other side would show your driver's license number on one corner, and a brief form enabling you to quickly report an instance of irresponsible driving behavior. To send a report you'd fill out the following form, affix a stamp and drop it in the mail.

The Motor Vehicle Department would record the information about the reported vehicle. Computers would collate the date monthly, quarterly or yearly. While the data would have no legal import, the information collected might be used in a number of ways.

Here is what the form might look like:

DRIVER SAFETY REPORT CARD — 1996

Date _____

Location_____

Car color/make/license_____

Infraction: Speeding ____ Weaving____

    Tailgating ____ Cutting off ____ Reckless ____

    Failure To Yield Right-Of-Way ____

    Other _____

Here are some suggested uses for the collected data:

- When an auto is reported twenty times, say, for tailgating, the car owner would be sent notification of this fact.
- When the same auto is reported thirty times for the

same offense, a state policeman would investigate. I would predict that for most drivers, the notification and investigation would, in themselves, cause them to modify their behavior.

- A state highway patrolman stopping a car for speeding could check Motor Vehicle Department records through an in-car computer to ascertain whether other instances of irresponsible driving had been reported. The officer might learn, for example, that the same automobile had been reported fifteen times for recklessness, twelve times for weaving and eight times for cutting off. He could then question the driver about them.

- A parent might learn from the Motor Vehicle Department that his automobile had been observed speeding twenty times when, he, personally had not been driving the car. Thus, he would be alerted to risky driving practices of his teenage child.

- A suspect speeding from the scene of a crime might be reported by several motorists ignorant of the crime but each with a bit of knowledge of the route of the speeder. Police could check Safety Driver Report Cards to identify auto owners for questioning.

- A chronically hostile driver regularly reported for reckless driving and belligerent behavior could be identified and investigated long before he actually assaulted someone.

- An auto might be reported by twenty drivers during one day at various locations extending along one particular highway. Such a dramatic occurrence witnessed by numerous drivers could merit looking into by the police.

- Reports on a particular auto might gradually escalate over a period of months; July (2), August (5), September (3), October (8), November (9). This indication of deteriorating driving ability might be due to alcoholism, senility, stress or encroaching blindness. Investigation is warranted before an accident happens.

But the benefits of Driver Safety Report Cards extend beyond these specific examples. Public debate and awareness about them would have the effect of bringing the highways back into the community. Right now, from a psychological standpoint, the highways amount to our "Wild West" — they are not thought of as part of any town. Often, anything goes. Because of driver anonymity we are apt to behave in rude, inconsiderate and uncivilized ways, behavior we wouldn't countenance in ourselves if we were to meet that same person walking down the street, in a store or in church. The highways are "no man's land."

Public discussion about Driver Safety Report Cards would make drivers more aware of possible community censure while driving, and this greater consciousness would result in more responsible driving and fewer accidents.

Secondly, Driver Safety Report Cards would lessen drivers' feelings of frustration and powerlessness, when they witness someone driving dangerously. One report won't make a difference, but if most drivers who observe bad driving were to send in their reports, the careless person could be tracked down. In place of asking helplessly, "What can I do about it?" the witness could file a report, thereby gaining the satisfaction that he has done his part. In my own experience, I've had many instances when I'd have happily dropped a Driver Safety Report Card in the next mail box.

Here's an example:

While traveling home in bumper to bumper, rush our traffic, northbound on Connecticut's lovely, tree-lined Merritt Parkway, one member of a long line of cars, a red Mazda, impatient at joining the line behind me, passed me on my right. He went on to pass the car ahead of me on it's right, but there encountered a slower moving vehicle in the right lane. Instead of slowing down, the Mazda abruptly cut in front of the vehicle in front of me, forcing it to slow down to avoid a collision. We continued on for several miles that way, the Mazda driver having risked several lives, including mine, to gain two car lengths.

DRIVER SAFETY REPORT CARD — *1996*

Date _August 8, 4:00 p.m._

Location _Northbound Merritt near Greenwich_

Car color/make/license _Red Mazda - CT 888-777_

Infraction: Speeding ___ Weaving _x_

Tailgating ___ Cutting off _x_ Reckless _x_

Failure To Yield Right-Of-Way ___

Other x Endangerment

Minor incident? Yes. Potential for disaster? Yes! Will it help to report it? The answer to this is crucial to understanding the evidence from the new brain research. This evidence strongly suggests the more one reinforces all community values the less likely will there be major transgressions. It is my opinion that the new police practices in New York City, of arresting and interrogating offenders of minor laws like graffiti, urinating in public and public beer drinking, have reduced major crime.

We learn from experience, not from words. Words only have import if experience reinforces them. Otherwise, they are *mere* words, having no grounding in reality. Without consistent reinforcement, the child-pupil-citizen-driver cannot know whether something is true or not. A few examples will make this evident.

If a school doesn't reinforce the need for students to be on time and lets them wander in whenever they choose, will there be order in classrooms? Will a student have reason to doubt other "truths" the school teaches?

Why does an army insist that soldiers shine their shoes and dress correctly? What has that got to do with the teamwork required in fighting an enemy? Teamwork begins with and is built on reinforcement of "minor" values. An army not taught and expected to shine their shoes in basic training, will be less able to engage effectively in combat.

A community where minor values are not reinforced will have a high crime rate. A highway where minor laws aren't reinforced will have a high accident rate.

The Passive-Aggressor is as responsible for accidents as the Speeder. Both are hostile, but show it in different ways. One obstructs; the other pushes. Each becomes the other's "a-- h---." The Speeder finds the Passive-Aggressor infuriatingly obstructive; the Passive-Aggressor finds the Speeder, a tailgater, infuriatingly pushy. Each violates community values, and, if not curtailed, each will encourage others, through his example, to do the same.

WHAT'S THE DOWN SIDE?

Any new procedure like Driver Safety Report Cards needs to be debated, and potential abuses dealt with in the process of enacting such a suggestion into law. Could someone try to make trouble for a particular person by falsely reporting them? Unlikely, since each report card would have the reporting driver's license number, and the number of cards anyone could send would be limited to five, initially. Abuse of the process would have little chance of success.

Furthermore, since the worst thing that can happen to someone reported a critical number of times is an investigation, no real harm can be done. At this point we cannot say what will happen after the police investigate, but we can assume they will be guided by the customary rules of evidence.

But if there is no teeth to the idea of Drivers Safety Report Cards, how will it make a difference? As I have said, I believe behavior becomes modified through community consensus and censure. The build-up of community pressure, the debate, the notification process and the investigation are teeth enough. You don't have to beat someone to get compliance if you have taught them (and they have learned) to wash their hands before eating, to eat with good manners, to listen to others and to communicate effectively.

One way of proceeding would be to try it out for one year on a pilot basis, and the resulting data simply collected and looked at. Do significant patterns emerge or don't they? Do authorities then discern that such information could be helpful toward moving us toward a greater feeling of community?

I believe that we have within our grasp the power to curb highway hostility and it's consequences: violence, accidents, injury, illness and death. I have described how the individual can achieve this for himself, and some of the principles that can be applied to hostility in our culture. Of course, a journey of a thousand miles must begin with a single step. Let us start with the road … establishing a tradition there will pave the way for the longer journey.

13

Driving Yourself Healthy

"For every minute you are angry you lose sixty seconds of happiness."

Emerson

In 1983, I concluded that my driving habits risked my health. Racing to destinations, cursing lackadaisical drivers who slowed my rush and punishing people who "didn't know how to drive" not only no longer made sense, it elevated my blood pressure.

Using the methods described in this book, I began changing my attitudes. However, as success followed my efforts, I experienced, inexplicably, terribly sad and lonely feelings. Slowly, memories of my father drifted into my awareness. Twenty-seven years after his death, I grieved anew for him.

Memories of my father intertwine intimately with automobiles. When I was barely able to see over the dashboard, I sat on his lap as he drove. Enfolded by his arms and nestled against his chest, I felt secure, loved and important. In addition to comfort, the view of oncoming cars and the excitement conveyed by my father's arms as he turned the steering wheel to contend with them produced unforgettable recollections.

On those occasions my father conveyed his happiness through song: "Sweet Adeline," "Home On The Range" and "My Merry Oldsmobile." His favorite, "Moonlight Bay," I often still sing as I drive. Its haunting, sweet melody and lyrics may not be known to you:

> "We were sailing along
> On Moonlight Bay
> You could hear the voices singing,
> They seemed to say,
> You have stolen her heart
> Now don't go 'way
> As we sing love's old sweet song
> On Moonlight Bay."

When I grew older and my reach longer, my father let me "steer" while sitting on his lap. With still further growth, I could sit between his legs. From this position, I learned to work the clutch, shift gears and steer.

Finally, the day came when he pulled the car over to the side of an isolated country road.

"Okay," he said, "You drive."

My memory sings...there was the lowering sun bathing the fields and dirt road in gold as my father, watched by a few cows and accompanied by a meadowlark's song, walked around to the passenger side and coached me while I, tentatively, eased the car back on the road. What a thrill!

From that day on and for the four years prior to getting my driver's license, whenever I journeyed with my father I waited anxiously for the moment's return when, the day's business completed, he'd stop the car.

How I Changed

My father's way of driving became my way of driving. As long as I drove his way, he rode with me. Giving up his way of driving felt sad, as though I was separating myself from him.

"Sorry, Dad, I can't go along with you on this one. I need to go my own way."

To keep my connection to my father alive, I reflected on some other memory I could emphasize to replace the memories of fast, sometimes stressful driving. When he wasn't trying to make time, he would relax, sing and drive leisurely. I decided to replace the memory of my father's speeding by one emphasizing his singing. I wanted the car to be a place that facilitated the recollection of joyful time, not frantic ones.

To reinforce this, I set my radio on all the stations I liked best. If one station began a commercial, another, broadcasting music, was a finger jab away. I bought tapes of all my favorites: classical, marches, vocals, chamber music, country and western and choral groups. Different music for different moods. As I "use up" a CD or tape, I replace it with a new one.

I chose the singing Dad as my mentor, not the "driven" Dad.

We all have mentors. We all emulate someone when we drive. It may be a father, mother, uncle, aunt, brother or sister. Or it may be a sports figure, coach, racer or character in a movie. If the style of driving is injurious or potentially dangerous for us, we can choose to emulate that part which is healthier, as I did, or switch to another mentor.

Actually, I've done both. Besides switching to my singing father, I consciously choose to emulate the calm steadiness of the state trooper or airline pilot who never seem frayed, no matter what the circumstance. I like that feeling. It's much better than the intensity of an Indianapolis 500 driver!

Who is your mentor?

For men growing up in America, athletic coaches, military heroes and sports idols have been our principal mentors. Listening to the last Super Bowl, I heard, once again, the dictums of the coaching profession;

- Give 100 percent all the time.
- The one that wants it badly enough wins.
- When the going gets tough, the tough get going.
- Winning is everything.

These are terrific motivators for a three-hour sports contest. They are also excellent for specific projects, or where extra effort may mean the difference between success and failure.

However, if a person rigidly applies them to all aspects of life all of the time, they can eventually result in illness. Note the number of football coaches with heart attacks or who have had coronary artery by-pass operations.

One of the most common scenarios I hear from men with heart attacks is a history of nonstop work for weeks or months before it happened. The four dictums applied consistently to life lead to the grave:

"We worked night and day for three months straight."

"I worked afternoon and evening shifts six months."

"I accumulated 120 vacation days in twenty years."

"For the past three years, I've worked fourteen-hour days, and brought work home on weekends."

Moreover, these dictums actually *detract* from quality of life; men who pursue them exclusively end up robbed of certain mental capacities.

As I discussed earlier, most of us experience transient episodes in which our ability to be fully aware dims or disappears. I identified these episodes as five degrees of seeing and hearing. Sensory enjoyment can be diminished as you bring stress into your life.

During the course of a day, you may range through all five levels of seeing and hearing. However, as you spend more and more time using stress hormones while striving to reach goals, the range of your emotional response narrows. You rarely venture into level four, and never reach level five where you see and hear with relish and passion. Gradually, through disuse of the neuronal connection required for levels four and five, these connections wither. Eventually, you can't get them back.

Use it or lose it. There is *no* way around this fact: you *have* to live within your skin. When you are maximally exerting yourself, giving 100 percent, levels four and five are not attainable. You can't give your full attention to a Mozart flute concerto and speed through traffic at the same time. Our brains offer us polarities; every moment we choose a level of existence somewhere between one and five.

Health means retaining possession of our capability to range from one to five, maintaining full possession of our faculties. Ill health means we lose this ability. This can happen when we remain fixed in an extreme position for too long.

Charles Darwin, who spent his life in exhausting research, lamented, in his fifties, that he could no longer enjoy music, theater or poetry. Creativity, innovation and the ability to *feel* passion, joy and humor; to relish abstract nuances of meaning and to find peace and contentment when alone — *all these are lost* as a consequence of unremitting pursuit of competitive beliefs!

Applied to highway travel, the dictums of competition are ridiculous and they result in a tension-filled trip. Let's examine these dictums one at a time.

Give 100 percent all the time. That's impossible! Giving your best *some* of the time, requires opportunities to recharge *some* of the time. We need to loaf, rest, sleep, play, love, joke, gab, relax and meditate.

On the road, pushing your car 100 percent will tire you for very little gain. Instead, consider your trip time out from the rat race time to recharge.

The one who wants it most will win. It ain't necessarily so! Desire alone will not get you there. Intelligence, good judgement, knowledge, personal relationships and communication skills are just a few of the factors that are more important than desire.

Keeping yourself worked up while driving won't get you there any sooner than being relaxed. Loosen up, don't be so serious, laugh it up. (You may not come this way again!)

When the going gets tough the tough get going. Sometimes, yes; but sometimes the "tough" are wise and know when to stop! Executives who don't choose relaxing layovers on business trips out of town are more apt to suffer stress illness. Yes, persistence is important, but this must always be weighed against the risk to health and personal relationships. Like Malcolm Forbes, "toughness" *may* get you the most toys, but premature death may cancel your availability to play with them!

Driving long distances despite fatigue invites disaster. Dan, a forty-two-year-old salesman who had already suffered a severe heart attack, prided himself on driving from Connecticut to Florida, nonstop, using cigarettes and coffee to keep him awake. You can be almost certain that he'll never get to play with his grandchildren. Pace yourself and plan travel with frequent stops. When tired, stop for the night. Don't kill yourself!

Winning is everything. Impossible quest, doomed from the start! *We're all going to be number two or less in most things!* People who actually believe this dictum will spend a lifetime hanging their heads, feeling like failures. Winning is not everything. The exaltation and public recognition from being "the champ" lasts only a moment. To guarantee happiness you should love what you're doing, whether you're number one or number 258,820,961!

"Winning" on the road has no real value. The highway is too dangerous for games. Pleasurable traveling depends on the mood *inside* your car, not your "rank" outside. Make your journey heavenly. Competing with yourself or others will make it hell.

These four dictums are as American as apple pie. The Speeder and the Competitor represent the expression of these four dictums when they are applied to driving a car. The problem with them is that when they are followed blindly, they cause illness and death. More is not necessarily better. Faster is not necessarily better. Winning is not necessarily better.

A common sequence seen in cartoons depicts some character — a rabbit, fox or other small animal — running so fast that he runs beyond the edge of a cliff and continues for some distance even though he has no ground under him. At that point he notices where he is, and at the moment of awareness, he plummets to the canyon below.

That's the fate of the Speeder and the Competitor. That's the fate of the blind followers of the four dictums. Health requires balance. This book is about restoring that balance. You cannot be fully alive, experiencing all five levels of the glorious sensory experience available to you, unless you have that balance. You can begin to acquire that balance as you drive your automobile.

You can drive yourself healthy!

Make one more three-by-five card. Pick a mentor who embodies the ideals you want and fill it out:

Old Belief

Stressor:	Living up to a mentor.
Urge:	Rush
	Drive like my dad, rushing.
	Give 100 percent all the time.
	The one who wants it the most wins.
	When the going gets tough the tough get going.
	Winning is everything.

On the other side, write:

New Belief

Event:	Choosing a mentor
Urge:	Relish life

Drive like my dad, singing.
Drive like an airline pilot.
Driving is recharge time.
Loosen up, lighten up.
You may never go this way again.

With practice you can change. Charley did. A highly successful financial adviser, he once described a journey he and his wife made to Boston from Fairfield, Connecticut.

"Initially, we had bumper to bumper traffic, which made it very difficult to make good time. Then just out of Hartford, we ran into the damnedest traffic jam you ever saw. A tractor-trailer had gone off the road. Once on the Massachusetts Turnpike it was pretty smooth sailing, except for some jackass, who tried to cut me off around Worcester. But apart from that, the rest of the trip was all *non-events*. We still made it to Boston in three hours."

Non-events! What were these non-events? Conversations with his wife? Games with his children? Music? Scenery along the turnpike? The gentle ride of his luxury automobile? He made the trip at sensory levels one and two. He was dead to the remainder of his experience.

Charley's limited perceptiveness extended beyond the car. For years his hobby had been surf fishing. Frequently, he rose early in the morning and drove down to the Connecticut shore where he joined other fishermen casting in the surf for fish. But Charley didn't speak about enjoying himself; he paid attention only to the number and size of his catch and how it stacked up to that of other fishermen.

Despite fishing with the same men for years, he did not know their last names, where they lived, marital status, if they had children or telephone numbers. He made no effort to initiate friendships, even to meet anyone off the beach for coffee! (All non-events?)

During the year or so that I knew Charley, he changed dramatically. Like many stressed, bright individuals I've worked with, once he applied his intellectual gifts to understanding his stress response, change came rapidly. Now he speaks of his joy watching the sun rise over the sea as he slips into his waders at the Connecticut shore. He loves the salt air, the sound of the gulls and the beauty of the surf.

That special rough-and-ready bonding that men have — the kind I learned from my father — the bull-----ing, joke-telling, and good-natured teasing interest Charley almost as much as catching the biggest fish. He's making friends at get-togethers off the beach.

"Non-events" have become prime events with his family, too. He enjoys the "child" in his children *and* himself. On another trip to Boston, two years after the one described, he made a point of stopping at Sturbridge Village, a replica of a colonial community halfway between Fairfield County and Boston. The casual tour and snack gave Charley and his family something to look forward to, something to experience and learn from and something to talk about afterward, as the ideas and associations planted through the visit took root and grew.

In place of living to work, Charley has begun working to live.

Recently, I found this poem. The author is unknown.

Yesterday is history,
Tomorrow is a mystery,
Today is a gift.
That's why it's called the present.

Each automobile journey can be a gift you give yourself and your companions. I'd like to share some poignant memories which may stir some of your own:

Montauk Point. One summer night in Manhattan, I had my first date with the woman who would become my wife. Following a dinner in a French restaurant, we strolled to my car, parked under a streetlight, embraced and kissed for the first time. We were overcome by an extraordinary rapture. Not wanting the night to end, we decided to travel to Montauk Point at the tip of Long Island to watch the sun come up. Never mind that it was almost midnight, never mind that Montauk was hours away, we wanted to start our journey together, and we wanted to start now.

It was a blissfully unforgettable night. The passion and energy from our new love transported us into some magical surreal state in which the car seemed to drift along in a stream of traffic like a boat on a gentle winding river.

We never made Montauk. Sometime before dawn we drove into the empty parking lot at the Robert P. Moses State Beach about a quarter of the way to Montauk, found our way to some sand, wrapped ourselves in blankets, and slept joyfully until wakened by the sound of early morning beach-goers wending their way through the misty haze to their places along the shore.

I had never known such ecstacy.

Berkshires. Another summer we drove along a rolling road in the Western Massachusetts Berkshires, the deep lush green trees forming cozy, intimate tunnels for us to pass through. Between myself and my wife stood our drowsy, two-year-old firstborn, resolutely determined to stay awake. She and I exchanged smiling, knowing glances as the familiar scenario unfolded. His eyes finally closed though he remained standing. Gently she lifted him, lay him down so his head rested on my lap, and his legs draped over hers. She covered him with a light blanket. We held hands and continued our journey.

Vermont. The same boy, now four, with me in the car — just us guys traveling toward Newfane, Vermont to hunt deer with bow and arrow. Though his arrow had a rubber-tipped suction cup, his excitement while discussing his first "hunt" was contagious. In a scene reminiscent of many with my father, we started off before dawn from our home in Longmeadow, Massachusetts, and as we crossed the Vermont line, lights along the road began to wink off. The sky began to brighten when we stopped for sweet rolls. By the time we reached our destination, a small field at the end of a dirt road a few miles north of Newfane, other hunters arrived, quietly got their gear together, and stealthily disappeared into the woods.

We soon followed; not so quietly, not so stealthily, but as excited as all of them combined. We stopped to pee, we stopped to eat a Fig Newton, we stopped to discuss the habits of deer, and we stopped to rest.

The dear I sought came with me.

Canada. Returning from a skiing vacation in Canada, my wife and I in the front seat, our seven-year-old son and five-year-old daughter in the back seat, we sang songs together. First came the Big Ten football songs. Next, we tackled some rounds of, "Three Blind Mice," and "Row, Row, Row Your Boat." Following that, the *oldies,* "Home On The Range," "Dinah," "Sweet Adeline," "Down By The Old Mill Stream," and "Moonlight Bay."

We were all incredibly happy.

Connecticut. Late winter in an empty schoolyard parking lot in Westport I repeated a memory with my son I had first experienced with my father. The inch of new snow that had fallen during the night was just beginning to melt under a bright morning sun, as I drove into the lot, stopped the car, and said to my ten-year-old youngest son, "Okay. You drive."

I walked around to the passenger side, got in, opened the lid on my cup of coffee, and, as I had done with his brother and sister, coached him as he eased the car into black zigzag tracings over the fresh snow. The morning sun sparkled off the snow etched trees. Great coffee.

I have many lively memories of motoring in America, driving along lonely and crowded highways not to win a contest, but to enjoy the ride and the pleasure of the company with me. I'm so glad I turned my back on the kind of frenzied driver I used to be, for now I can appreciate and practice what Walt Whitman meant when he wrote:

"Afoot and light hearted
I take to the open road,
Healthy, free, the world before me,
A long brown path
Leading wherever I choose."

14

Driving In Another World

---

*"Oh, beauty before me, beauty behind me, beauty
to the right of me, beauty to the left of me, beauty
above me, beauty below me, I'm on the pollen path."*
Navajo Saying

Lucy, my dinner companion, learning of my interest in
highway stress, said to me, "Haven't you noticed that
there has been an increase in rudeness and outright
nastiness on the highway lately?"

"Perhaps that is so," I replied, "but, my own experience is that it has been less."

What I didn't say is that I find it has been practically
non-existent. Now, how do you square Lucy's experience
and mine? Are we driving in the same world?

Of course I know Lucy's world exists; if it didn't I
wouldn't have written this book. Sometimes I observe it:
Driving to Philadelphia with my wife during the Christmas
Holiday 1995, to attend the Brancusi exhibit at the

Philadelphia Museum of Art, we saw a Jeep station wagon careening in the middle lane of the New Jersey Turnpike, embroiled in a battle for supremacy with a sports car. I gave it very wide berth, dropping back away from the Jeep which looked like it might go out of control. But I didn't feel involved with it like I used to be. I didn't say they shouldn't allow them on the road. And while there were probably a hundred examples of nastiness and rudeness during the drive to Philadelphia and back the next day, this was the only one I took any notice of and remember.

Sometimes I re-experience what Lucy referred to. Sometimes, I step back into the highway world I used to inhabit, and the world my father introduced me to. That occurs only when I feel I am going to be late for an important appointment. Since I usually allow myself fifty percent more time than my estimated driving time and never drive over two hours at a stretch or four hours a day, I rarely get tired and cross while driving.

The particular world we experience around us depends on which areas of our brains have become activated. There is no "true" reality, all is an individually interpreted reality. We cannot escape from this feature of our basic biological make-up. Remember my description of "car wash magic?" In the space of ten minutes my highway world changed from the rude one Lucy talked about (and one I usually inhabited in those days) to a courteous one. This wasn't due to a change in the way others drove — it came from a change in me. My brain had tuned in to hear another music.

My highway world changed permanently during the six years it took me to write this book. Take a moment and re-read the first pages of the chapter on Angry Drivers, up to "How Angry Can You Get?" What sort of feelings are stimulated in you? Then re-read the last pages of the preceding chapter, Driving Yourself Healthy from "Montauk Point" to the end of the chapter. What kind of feelings does that stimulate in you?

You'll notice my mood, conveyed through my writing, differs in the two pieces. As you read so might yours in response to mine. You can see and experience each of the two worlds. The first piece, written six years ago reflects my more combative attitude; while the second reflects a focus on beauty, as expressed so movingly by the Navajo.

The reason there are two worlds grows out of the core nature of our biological make-up. Our brains, where our decision-making processes are centralized, consist of billions of neurons, each of which either fires or does not fire. None "sorta" fire. Each switch is either "on" or "off." Consequently, what we experience each moment of our lives is the product of millions of "either-or" synaptic decisions. Each synaptic decision represents our brain's response to and is derived from an amazing computer-like analysis of the interplay of data coming from our senses, the memory of previous information, experience and our genetic endowment.

Now, that's a mouthful!

Dr. Rudolfo Llinas, professor of neuroscience at New York University, expressed it more poetically: "A person's waking life is a dream guided by the senses."

But these are not isolated neuronal firings. The neurons are in modular groups, each specializing in different sensory inputs along a certain continuum. For example, certain modules register shades of black and white; others sweet to bitter; others loud to soft. Of course, none of these three polarities bear directly on highway stress. I mention them because they're apt to be familiar to you, and will make what I'm talking about more understandable.

One major continuum that is linked directly to highway madness is trust versus mistrust: is the person (or situation) friend or foe, safe or dangerous, positive or negative. It's readily apparent that our brains must constantly make a determination along this continuum; we could not survive without it. It's basic, and it supersedes all other brain polarities. While a polarity like "sweet or bitter" is not stimulated into action until you put food into your mouth, (except as metaphor) "trust or mistrust" and the variants of it listed above, come into play whenever we open our eyes and begin our day.

During our earliest stages of life we learn to trust or mistrust, and our parents emphasize what's safe and what's dangerous. We cannot afford not to make this calculation.

Dr. Paul Churchland, in his book about the brain, *The Engine of Reason, The Seat of the Soul,* describes how the brain computes the many vectors that go into such evaluations through complex feedback and feed forward circuits. It's a ceaseless activity of our brains all our lives.

If, as the result of such assessment, our brain concludes mistrust-threat-danger, stress hormones pour out, mobilizing our vigilance and making us more alert so we can contend with the threat, ready to fight or flee. On the other hand, if our brain concludes trust-friend-safe, endorphins pour out, mobilizing our ability to love and embrace.

There, dear reader, you have the two worlds! Whichever "world" our brain's biological mechanism concludes we are facing at any given moment ... that's the one we're living in.

Sometimes highways *are* more dangerous. Driving into downtown Philadelphia on an unfamiliar expressway during evening rush hour, looking for the turnoff to the Philadelphia Museum of Art, had both my wife and me very anxious. Decisions had to be made in split seconds, or we'd miss our exit and have to travel unknown extra miles.

Other times highways *are* tranquil, even boring. Last summer, vacationing in Montana, Wyoming and Idaho, we drove for miles on straightaways with scarcely another car in sight, free to talk and gaze at the wondrous scenery.

But both of these situations are rare; they're not the principle object of our concern even though the principles put forward in this book will reduce the stress in the Philadelphia-type situation, and increase the pleasure in Montana.

The point I'm making is that highway stress escalating into highway madness stems not from the highway conditions, per se, but from the values-beliefs-attitudes drivers hold towards themselves, other drivers and individuals responsible for the road conditions.

The consequences for the drivers holding those five values-beliefs-attitudes which have been the primary focus of this book are having a grossly exaggerated sense of mistrust-threat-danger; their highway world abounds with rudeness and nastiness.

These values-beliefs-attitudes can be changed without impairing your ability to skillfully drive your car. On the contrary, changing the attitudes will increase your ability to operate your vehicle safely and skillfully. You won't be so distracted, impatient or impulsive.

What's more, when you make the changes, the highway world will be experienced as a better place. It's an amazing experience when you first drive in the more courteous, friendlier world. It seems too good to be true.

Why is this so? How do the five beliefs I've described create a false sense of mistrust-threat-danger?

Consider for example, the Speeder's dictum, "Make Good Time." As long as he continues to set a fixed driving time, he will perceive any circumstance that likely interferes with accomplishing that objective as a *threat*. Anytime we have a personal investment in something, be it as important as our very lives, or as trivial as our driving time, our brains will compute mistrust-threat-danger, if the object of our affection might be lost. It all depends on the strength and intensity of our investment.

The relationship of mistrust-threat-danger to the values of the Competitor and the Passive-Aggressor are even easier to understand. Each visualizes other drivers and opponents as downright enemies. Drivers with these attitudes are going to fight — a lot. Moreover, they will constantly define each encounter as a win-lose situation. Consequently, self-esteem is forever at stake. This mobilizes enough adrenaline and other stress hormones to empower a gladiator in the Roman Coliseum.

The Narcissist perceives anyone who is not like himself, either in appearance or behavior, as a threat. Consequently, his world is full of "a-- h---s," and he drives full of rage. The world view of the Narcissist (They shouldn't allow them on the road.) reflects an exaggerated response to the "unfamiliar." Our brains develop step by step, and in early childhood, narcissism is a normal first stage; we *are* self-absorbed, only gradually enlarging our circle of trust. We come to trust the familiar; we don't trust the unfamiliar. Throughout life, psychological growth consists of converting the unfamiliar into the familiar. In this sense, aspects of narcissism are always with us, but with maturation we realize that that which seems unfamiliar contains opportunities as much or more than it portends threats.

On the highway you can notice a manifestation of this narcissism by being aware of your greater feeling of comfort with drivers of cars of the same make as your own. If the vehicle is identical to yours you may be tempted to wave. On the other hand, if there is a make, model or color of car you don't like, you will experience a less friendly, more suspicious attitude toward the driver. The extent to which we equate difference with threat determines which world we drive in.

A Vigilante is a Narcissist with a club. He is prepared to make all the a-- h---s shape up. He further escalates his perception of mistrust-threat-danger into "enemy" and actually goes to war, either verbally or physically to try to eliminate the stranger or his behavior. The Vigilante is a "Road Warrior," and he lives farthest from my new world.

By changing these values as I have proposed, we move from a world of danger and threat into a world of opportunity and beauty. By deciding to focus on "Making time good," in place of "Making good time" you remove a consideration that will cast a pall over your whole driving experience and replace it with a determination to maximize enjoyment. By deciding to focus on indulging yourself in place of making up competitions with others, you're guaranteed enhanced self-esteem. By developing a compassionate attitude towards others on the road, giving them the benefit of the doubt, letting them live and let live, and leaving punishment to the police you free your energies for living life fully.

Crossing over from the war path to the beauty path requires not only changing these beliefs cognitively, but coming to hold them with conviction, to really take them to heart. How do you develop conviction? To take this final step in your highway transformation, it will be helpful to understand more about the nature of the brain, particularly regarding polarities, vectors and somatic markers.

Much popular music springs from the recognition of the "choice" our brains constantly make about polarities. One example of this is the song, "Sunny Side of the Street." As you read the lyrics and "hear" the music most of you will notice that your mood will lighten. The song will enable you to move from one world towards the other. Of course, if you don't know the music, the effect of the lyrics will be smaller. And, if you are really in a grouchy, depressed or angry mood, you might even feel worse; your present circumstances may be such a powerful determinate, bringing you to the conclusion that your world is a dark place, that a mere song won't change your mind.

> Grab your coat and get your hat,
> Leave your worries on the doorstep,
> Just direct your feet
> To the sunny side of the street.
> Don't you hear the pitter pat
> And the hurried step is your beat,
> Life can be so sweet,
> On the sunny side of the street.
> I used to walk in the shade
> With those blues on parade,
> But I'm not afraid,
> This rover, crossed over.
> If I never had a cent
> I'd be rich as Rockefeller,
> Gold dust at my feet,
> On the sunny side of the street.

Most of you, in reading this, will experience a slight or significant shift in your mood. This mood may stay with you until the memory of the music begins to fade. Gradually, the mood will fade, too. But it illustrates the power of cognitive stimuli paired with emotional conditioning to move you a little from my father's world towards my new world. The methods you are learning are far more powerful and longer lasting than this song; they have to be, your resistance to change can be strong.

Dr. Antonio Damosio, Professor of Neurology at the University of Iowa College of Medicine, in his illuminating book, *Descartes' Error,* clearly describes the role of emotion in our brain's ability to arrive at conclusions and reach decisions. Damosio points out the role of what he terms "somatic markers" in reaching conclusions; most of our decisions are not made on the basis of "reason" alone. Here are two examples:

First, consider speaking a profanity, one of those you might readily say about a tailgater, for instance, while standing before an altar in a place of worship. Even if you say to yourself, "I don't mean it. This is only an experiment suggested by a book. God will understand," the words won't come out, or if they do, they will be severely muted. You may experience a feeling of revulsion and horror (the somatic marker) and a thought that lightning might come from above and strike you dead (the cognitive thought stimulated by the somatic marker). In the days following your remark, you may attribute any misfortune that befalls you or your family to having spoken a four-letter word. Logic and reason are feeble counters, just by themselves, to emotional conditioning.

Another experiment: late at night when the streets are

clear and you know it's perfectly safe and there are no police around, drive through an intersection when the stoplight is red. The same thing happens: reason alone won't allow us to easily escape our biological conditioning, and most people, if they succeed in actually driving through the intersection, will immediately feel guilty (a somatic marker) and look around for the police (a cognitive thought stimulated into awareness by the somatic marker) who may have been watching from a distance.

The power of somatic markers is awesome. I read an account in an authoritative scientific journal about a Haitian man, a devout believer in voodoo, who believed that if he ate chicken he would die. One evening, a friend who thought voodoo was nonsense secretly served the man chicken, contained in a stew with other meats and vegetables. A year after the meal, to demonstrate to the Haitian the groundlessness of his fear, he told him the truth about the stew's ingredients.

"Now do you see how stupid your superstitions are? You didn't die after you ate chicken and it's been over a year," he said triumphantly. Then, within moments, he watched in horror as the Haitian collapsed and died, a victim of cardiac arrest, brought on by an enormous outpouring of adrenaline.

Our brains are no different than the Haitian man's, in terms of the basic biological structure of the brain. We differ only in terms of the *particular* cognitive beliefs learned and the *particular* somatic markers conditioned. Most of us do not believe in voodoo, but for many of you reading this book, swearing in a place of worship or driving through a red light will be no more consciously possible than eating chicken was for the Haitian.

However, no matter how strong the somatic markers

that trigger highway madness seem, even though the intensity of your anger at "bad" driving feels unchangeable, I have yet to meet the person who can't change. These aspects of your personality can change. It's not any harder than learning to improve your tennis game (or any game), learning a new language, learning the customs of a new country, or learning to drive your vehicle in the first place.

What makes it easy is knowing *what* to change. If you only focus on your anger and your justification for being angry at a particular driver, you won't change. If you fucus on changing the five handmaidens of highway madness, and the beliefs that maintain them *and,* if you de-condition yourself to the somatic markers, it will be very difficult for you *not* to change. Changing our attitudes and embracing new points of view can come about through the following five procedures:

First, change all of the vectors you can that bear on the mistrust-threat-danger versus trust-friend-safe polarity by making use of the three-by-five cards you made. That means all five beliefs simultaneously. A little bit of each one every day. Why is it important to work on all five at once? Because they're all linked and mutually reinforce each other.

It's really no different than learning to improve your tennis game. Hitting the ball can't be learned in isolation. You need to learn how to plant your feet, hold the racquet, watch the ball, etc.

Remember the neurons in the brain either fire or they don't fire. They don't "sorta" fire. Neurons receive either excitatory signals or inhibitory signals. The vigor of the response of any set of neurons to a given stimulus is determined by the number of neurons in the set that are stimulated enough to fire. If only half the members of the team are motivated to play, the total team's effort will be halved. Similarly, how angry you get, how clearly you see, or how passionately you feel are determined by how many of the neurons in that particular set or module are stimulated enough to fire. This, in turn, depends on the net effect of all the excitatory and inhibitory stimuli impinging on them.

Since all five beliefs contribute to the mistrust-threat-danger versus trust-friendly-safe polarity — the more you change, the better you feel.

Second, *memorize!* In order to hold the new beliefs with conviction, you must convert them from short term memory to long term memory. That way they really, indeed literally, become *part* of you: new brain neuronal connections take place and your gray matter *grows*. Read the new beliefs each morning soon after awakening and before you drive off, then again before going to sleep, imagining situations where they are relevant. This takes only a few minutes.

You know the names attached to the five driving attitudes. Without looking at your card, try to recall the new beliefs you need to change Speeder. Don't make learning a competition, either. Simply note how many you remembered, then look at the card, refresh your memory, put the card away then try to recall again. Repeat this three times each day with each card. This will take less than five minutes. In time, you will remember them all. Think of the number of people's names you remember. What makes it seem hard is your resistance to changing your point of view.

It is not possible to memorize these new beliefs and not change.

The only way you can remain as angry as you are is to remain ignorant. Knowledge is power!

Third, practice, practice, practice. Reread the new beliefs and try to remember them each time you slip back into the old attitudes, bringing them into play at the appropriate time. In learning how to improve your tennis game, you might ask a pro to help you. He watches you play, and at a certain point he may say, "No, not that way, do it this way." You go back over the stroke with the new belief in mind.

Don't be hard on yourself if you have trouble learning or if you keep forgetting. Don't give up if after an initial improvement you have a day when you revert back to Mr. Hyde. Rome wasn't built in a day, but Rome was built. You can change, too. Be patient with yourself.

Four, incorporate the new beliefs by precise timing. You learn a new sequence of thoughts to replace the old ones. In tennis the eye of the tennis player sees the ball, the brain calculates the distance and *at a certain point* initiates the new thought, then the swing. In learning a new language, the eye of the French student sees the house, the brain calculates the appropriate moment and initiates the new word and then the vocal apparatus speaks it: "maison." The eye of the stressed driver sees the stressor, and at the appropriate moment initiates the new thought and then the new driving behavior.

What is the appropriate moment? The time should occur as closely as possible to the point where a sequence of thoughts is just about ready to trigger the stress response. At that point the new thoughts rush in and the stress response is thwarted.

When you find yourself erupting in the old manner, ask yourself which set of values was involved. Were you trying to make good time, trying to beat someone, or had you just decided you didn't like something about the other guy? At that point, go over the pertinent new set of beliefs. Try to memorize them right on the spot, then again an hour after you arrive home and have had time to cool down. Make a special point of reviewing that night before going to bed, and the next morning before setting off.

Put the relevant card in a prominent place on your dashboard where you can easily keep it in view.

I believe this part is essential to overcoming the somatic marker.

Five, persist! Within a month, if you are persistent in your practice, you will notice a shift toward the new world, and by three months *you won't go back* (except for brief occasional lapses).

The key is to remember that most other drivers are just like you: well-intentioned human beings, hoping to live out their all too brief lives in relative peace and harmony. But like the old you, they may have misguided beliefs. In dealing with those "unconverted," spend some time contemplating these concluding words from Thornton Wilder's book, *The Bridge of San Luis Rey:*

"There is the land of the living and a land of the dead, and the bridge is love."

15

Driver's Stress Profile

Take the test before reading the book and one month after reading the book, memorizing the new beliefs and practice, practice, practice.

Answer each statement as honestly as you can. See pages 177-178 for scoring information. Score each statement that applies to you as follows:

Always - 3 — Often- 2 — Sometimes - 1 — Never - 0

I	Anger	Score
1.	Get angry at drivers.	____
2.	Get angry at fast drivers.	____
3.	Get angry at slow drivers.	____
4.	Get angry when cut off.	____
5.	Get angry at malfunctioning stoplights.	____
6.	Get angry at traffic jams.	____
7.	Spouse or friends tell you to calm down.	____

8.   Get angry at tailgaters.   _____
9.   Get angry at your passengers.   _____
10. Get angry when multilane highway narrows.   _____
     Total I: _____

II   Impatience
1.   Impatient waiting for passengers to get in.   _____
2.   So impatient, won't let car engine warm up.   _____
3.   Impatient at stoplights.   _____
4.   Impatient waiting in lines (car wash, bank).   _____
5.   Impatient waiting for parking space.   _____
6.   As passenger, impatient with driver.   _____
7.   Impatient when car ahead slows down.   _____
8.   Impatient if behind schedule on a trip.   _____
9.   Impatient driving in far right, slow lane.   _____
10. Impatient with pedestrians crossing street.   _____
     Total II: _____

III   Competing
1.   Compete on the road.   _____
2.   Compete with yourself.   _____
3.   Compete with other drivers.   _____
4.   Challenge other drivers.   _____
5.   Race other drivers.   _____
6.   Compete with cars in tollbooth lines.   _____
7.   Compete with other cars in traffic jams.   _____
8.   Compete with drivers who challenge you.   _____
9.   Compete to amuse self when bored.   _____
10. Drag race adjacent car at stop lights.   _____
     Total III: _____

IV **Punishing**

1. Do you "punish" bad drivers. ____
2. Complain to passengers about other drivers. ____
3. Curse at other drivers. ____
4. Make obscene gestures. ____
5. Block cars trying to pass. ____
6. Block cars trying to change lanes. ____
7. Ride another car's tail. ____
8. Brake suddenly to punish tailgater. ____
9. Use high beams to punish bad driver. ____
10. Seek personal encounter with bad driver. ____

Total IV: ____

Total of I, II, III, IV ____

SIGNIFICANCE OF DRIVER'S STRESS PROFILE

Answering honestly and accurately, you can obtain a measure of your hostility on the road. Since we tend to underestimate our reactivity, it may help to take this with a friend or spouse.

I Anger	Possible score	30
	High	15+
	Moderate	10-14
	Low	0-9

II Impatience	Possible score	30
	High	15+
	Moderate	8-14
	Low	0-7

III Competing	Possible score	30
	High	10+
	Moderate	5-9
	Low	0-4

IV Punishing	Possible score	30
	High	10+
	Moderate	5-9
	Low	0-4

Total	Possible score	120
	High	50+
	Moderate	28-49
	Low	0-27

DRIVER STRESS PROFILE RESULTS

Anger _____

Impatience _____

Competing _____

Punishing _____

Total _____

Epilogue

In this book I've focused on heart attacks, highway accidents and highway violence, and proposed that they are caused by five values-beliefs-attitudes residing in the driver's mind. When these beliefs are subscribed to and acted on these three tragedies are apt to occur.

The heart attack candidate experiences similar episodes of madness throughout his life. These are the crucial determinates that propel him toward a looming catastrophe. *The cause of heart disease does not reside in the heart!*

Unfortunately, most of our nation's health resources are poured into the treatment of only the final stage, coronary artery disease. But coronary artery disease has nothing to do with the basic problem. That's a strange sounding declaration, isn't it? But it happens to be true. It's as though we were to continue to treat yellow fever, but neglect draining the swamps where the mosquitoes, carrying the pathogenic virus, breed. The pathogen in coronary artery disease is not a virus but that doesn't make it any less a pathogen. As Dr. Meyer Friedman pointed out long ago, the pathogen is persistent and recurrent anger, irritation, aggravation and impatience. The swamps are the values-beliefs-attitudes which, when maintained, "breed" the pathogens.

For a fraction of the sum presently being thus expended, heart attacks before the age of seventy could be reduced by half within ten years. Heart attacks are a preventable illness!

The implications don't stop here. The cause of hypertension and migraine doesn't reside in the arteries, the cause of breast cancer doesn't reside in the breasts, the cause of Chrone's disease doesn't originate in the gut, the cause of diabetes doesn't reside in the pancreas, the cause of arthritis doesn't start in the joints, nor Parkinsonism in the cerebellum, nor Alzheimer's in brain tangles. Instead, for each disease, I feel that there are specific constellations of beliefs that precede the physical illness. Just as in heart disease, by ascribing to these beliefs, the individual's brain generates physiological consequences which cause the pathological changes associated with each condition.

In this sense, aside from diseases strongly influenced by genetics, infections, allergies and toxic reactions, *physical illness is a myth*. The illnesses described above (and more), are basically *mental illnesses that are expressed in physiological consequences* outside and inside the brain.

Fundamentally, they originate through the same brain dynamic mechanism as depression. Indeed, depression itself has physiologic changes associated with it, and when continued long enough, pathological organic alteration.

These are some of the rough psychological beliefs precipitating the illnesses below. For now, this list is solely designed to illustrate the continued application of this theory and enhance your ability to understand it.

Hypertension — Tremendous energy and anger directed toward achieving some goal, is kept secret, undisclosed and held in check.

Migraine — Anger, secondary to offensive remarks or behavior of another, gets directed into physical activity or tasks, until the accumulating rage causes spasm in cerebral arteries producing pain and physiologic aura.

Breast cancer — The inclination to nurture and soothe others, even those who attack, takes precedence over nurturing of self and self defense. Eventually, the nurturing organ gives out.

Chrone's disease — Anger due to abuse from a nurturing figure, like a parent, gets expressed passively through thwarting or disappointing that person. They are unable to perform for the person who abused them, even in their bowel function which was one of the first ways they did perform.

Diabetes — Nonstop physical and mental activity, oblivious to fatigue, results in depletion and eventual burnout of pancreatic cells.

Arthritis — Fear of taking physical action, literally, freezing from moving into action to express strong yearnings. Psychological freezing precedes joint freezing.

Parkinsonism — Inability to accept indications of early signs of what is perceived as mental or physical weakness, results in failure to address and get help for the "weakness." Pressing on, results in failure of brain to coordinate conflicting needs and drives. Failure of psychological coordination precedes failure of physiological coordination.

Alzheimer's — Unwillingness to engage in challenges

where one might fail or fall short, results in psychological withdrawal. Gradually the brain shuts down and a vicious cycle ensues. Psychological shut down precedes organic shut down.

This hypothesis suggests that treatment of these conditions requires changing the beliefs that determine the brain's "choices." As illustrated in this book, such beliefs may be changed by having the individual memorize and practice alternative new beliefs to replace the old ones. This requires skillful timing, but, fundamentally, the process illustrated throughout this book, is similar to learning a new language or tennis stroke. Timing, memorization and practice are essential.

The individual must acquire the skill to have access, mentally, to the new beliefs at precisely the moment when the choice of values-beliefs-attitudes is made by the brain in response to sensory cues. Then there has to be practice in follow through by taking action in the real world. With practice the new beliefs become entrenched, and the disease averted.

There are several other implications of this formulation.

First, we can change many characteristics of our own personalities.

Second, you can change someone against their will. For example, a person might not wish to become less enraged by drivers who cut in, but if he can be induced to memorize and practice the new beliefs described in this book (by financial incentives, for instance, or to get his driver's license back), he cannot help but become less angry when such incidents happen. The possibilities this holds for accident prevention and diminishing domestic violence, for example, are enormous.

Third, organizations that specialize in the treatment and prevention of specific diseases can launch educational campaigns designed to change the particular complex of values-beliefs-attitudes associated with a specific disease.

Fourth, prisons can introduce treatment approaches to change behavior instead of relying solely on punishment. Minds are not changed by punishment, they must have alternate options presented.

Farfetched? Try it out yourself in the miniature laboratory that is your automobile on the road. Follow these simple instructions:

1. Clearly identify the precise incident and internal cues that spark your anger or rage.
2. Write them down each time after they occur, estimating your anger from one to ten.
3. Using three-by-five cards, as described, memorize the five beliefs and their alternatives.
4. Determine which of the five beliefs is associated with each type of incident you overreact to.
5. Practice recalling the new belief each morning and before sleep, and at the precise moment when the incident and internal cues happen; first, in your imagination, then when the incident begins to unfold, and again just after the event.

You need to be motivated to practice, and to learn. You don't need to be motivated to change (of course it helps, and most of you would not have read this far without a wish to enjoy the road more), but the change from highway madness to highway pleasure comes automatically.

The possible applications of this phenomenon are limitless.

Afterword

My own father did not live to read this book. I'm sure the psychological forces described here contributed significantly to his illness and death. My hope is that readers will learn as I did from his mistakes.

To measure your progress, retake the Driver's Stress Test one month after finishing the book, after you've had a chance to practice the new attitudes.

We are all on the road of life. Happy motoring!

Bibliography

Benson, Herbert, *The Relaxation Response,* Avon Paperbacks, New York, NY.

Benson, Herbert, *Beyond The Relaxation Response,* Times Books, New York, NY.

Bly, John, *Iron John,* Addison Wesley, 1990, Reading, MA.

Chopra, Deepak, *Quantum Healing,* Bantam Books, 1989, New York, NY.

Churchland, Paul, *The Engine Of Reason, The Seat Of The Soul,* MIT Press, 1995, Cambridge, MA.

Cousins, Norman, *The Healing Heart,* W.W. Norton Company, 1993, New York, NY.

Crick, Francis, *The Astonishing Hypothesis,* New York, Charles Scribner's Sons, 1993, New York, NY.

Damasio, Antonio R., *Descartes' Error,* G.P. Putnam's Sons, 1994, New York, NY.

Dennett, Daniel C., *Consciousness Explained,* Little, Brown and Company, 1991, Boston, MA.

Edleman, Gerald M., *Bright Air, Brilliant Fire,* BasicBooks, 1992, New York, NY.

Eliot, Robert S., *Is It Worth Dying For?,* Bantam Books, 1984, New York, NY.

Erikson, Joan, *Wisdom And The Senses,* W.W. Norton Company, 1988, New York, NY.

Friedman, Meyer and Ulmer, D., *Treating Type A Behavior And Your Heart,* Alfred A. Knopf, 1985, New York, NY.

Freudenberger, Herbert, *Burnout,* Bantam Paperback, 1980, New York, NY.

Gawain, Shakti, *Creative Visualization,* Bantam Paperback, 1982, New York, NY.

Goleman, Daniel, *Emotional Intelligence,* Bantam Books, 1995, New York, NY.

Kuhn, Thomas S., *The Structure Of Scientific Revolutions,* The University of Chicago Press, 1970, Chicago, IL.

Leshan, Lawrence, *You Can Fight For Your Life,* M. Evans Paperback, 1976, New York, NY.

Linas, Rudolpho R., *The Biology Of The Brain,* W. H. Freeman and Company, 1989, New York, NY.

Moyers, Bill, *Healing And The Mind,* Doubleday, 1995, New York, NY.

Ornish, Dean, *Reversing Heart Disease,* Random House, 1990, New York, NY.

Ornish, Dean, *Stress, Diet And Your Heart,* New American Library1984, New York, NY.

Restak, Richard M., *The Modular Brain,* Charles Scribner's Sons, 1994, New York, NY.

Rose, Steven, *The Making Of Memory,* Doubleday, 1993, New York, NY.

Roskies, Ethel, *Stress Management For The Healthy Type A,* Guilford Press, 1987, New York, NY.

Siegal, Bernie, *Love, Medicine and Miracles,* Harper and Rowe, 1986, New York, NY.

Siegal, Bernie, *Peace, Love And Healing,* Harper and Rowe, 1989, New York, NY.

Simonton, Carl O., *Getting Well Again,* Bantam Paperback, 1978, New York, NY.

Williams, Redford, *The Trusting Heart,* Times Books, 1989, New York, NY.

Williams, Redford and Williams, Virginia, *Anger Kills,* Times Books, 1993, New York, NY.

To order additional copies of

Steering Clear Of Highway Madness

Please send _____ copies at $14.95 for each book,
plus $3.50 shipping and handling for each book.

Enclosed is my check or money order of $_____
or [ ] Visa   [ ] MasterCard
#_____ Exp. Date ____/____
Signature _____

Name _____
Street Address _____
City _____
State _____ Zip _____
Phone _____

(Advise if recipient and shipping address are
different from above.)

For credit card orders call:
1-800-895-7323

or
Return this order form to:

BookPartners
P.O. Box 922
Wilsonville, OR 97070